The Historical Road of Anglicanism

The Historical Road of Anglicanism

Carroll E. Simcox
editor
The Living Church

Henry Regnery Company · Chicago

Other books by the author

LIVING THE CREED
LIVING THE LORD'S PRAYER
LIVING THE TEN COMMANDMENTS
THE WORDS OF OUR WORSHIP
UNDERSTANDING THE SACRAMENTS
THE PROMISES OF GOD
THEY MET AT PHILIPPI
IS DEATH THE END?
AN APPROACH TO THE EPISCOPAL CHURCH
THE FIRST GOSPEL
LIVING THE LOVE OF GOD

To
Fathers Roger, Alfred and Gerald
of the Order of St. Benedict—
friends of unforgotten years
and brothers in the one Lord,
one Faith, and one Baptism.

Author's Preface

A very patriotic Englishman once described his nation as a race of splendid mongrels. He saw his countrymen as a mixture of Celtic mysticism, Scandinavian stamina, Teutonic diligence, French verve and Roman statecraft, all adding up to something splendid in his judgment. He was, as I said, very patriotic. There are those who might put a quite different valuation on this English "mongrelism." Nevertheless, one cannot deny the fact of the extraordinary mixture of ethnic groups and cultural encounters in English history. It is one of the basic facts of that history. And what is true of the people of England is true of the Church of England, which has shared in the nation's mixing and blending process through the seventeen hundred years of its history. The historical road of Anglicanism is a road on which we meet many diverse travelors. By traversing that road in our historical imagination we may come to some understanding of that complex and heterogeneous form of Christianity known as Anglicanism. By this I mean specifically the faith and order found in the Churches of the Anglican Communion, that world-wide fellowship of Churches which derive from the Church of England as their mother, or, in some cases, their grandmother.

From the beginning of our age of grace, sagacious men have wagged their heads and said that some things, such as Jewish religion and Greek philosophy, simply cannot mix, that a working union of such incompatibles is unthinkable. So the Church—born in Palestine, educated in Greece, organized in Rome—is unthinkable, but there it is. The Anglican portion of the Church is scandalously laden with incompatibilities within, but there it is; and its devoted members believe, not unreasonably I hope since I am one of them, that this is because with God all things are possible and it is His doing.

I have written this book with Christians of other Churches primarily in mind, but I don't pretend to be impartial. Recently a graduate student in one of our universities, a Mormon, submitted a doctoral dissertation on the history of Mormonism. Asked by one of the examiners if he considered himself sufficiently unprejudiced to write objectively of Mormon history, he replied both bravely and prudently: "Yes, if you, not a Mormon, consider yourself unprejudiced enough to examine it." And so say I.

My sole purpose is to explain, describe, and inform, not to refute, argue, or proselytize. Job pleaded: "Let me be weighed in an even balance!" (Job 31:6) I make the same plea on behalf of that blessed company of faithful people in which God has placed me—the Anglican Communion.

Carroll E. Simcox

Table of Contents

Author's Preface		vii
A Chronological Table of Persons and Events		xi
1	Dawn	1
2	Celt, Saxon and Roman	8
3	A Century of Planting	14
4	The Vikings	21
5	Crown and Papacy	28
6	To the Great Charter	35
7	The Great Frustration	46
8	Medieval Religion	54
9	The Flaring of Mankind	64
10	The King's Matter	73
11	Revolution	83
12	Counter-Revolution	91
13	The Elizabethan Settlement	97
14	The Via Media	105
15	The King Supreme	115
16	The Royal Martyr	122
17	The Caroline Divines	129
18	Commonwealth and Restoration	138
19	The Age of Reason	146
20	Evangelicalism	155
21	The New World	163
22	Reform	172

23 The Catholic Revival   178
24 The Lively Victorians   185
25 The American Church   193
26 The Anglican Communion   202
27 Anglicanism and Reunion   209
28 Today and Tomorrow   216
Appendix   223
Bibliography   233

A Chronological Table of Persons and Events

Date		Page
c. 305	Martyrdom of St. Alban	3
c. 400	Pelagius *floruit*	4
432	Consecration of St. Patrick	5
563	Foundation of Iona community	6
590	Gregory becomes pope	10
597	Augustine reaches Britain	10
664	Synod of Whitby	12
669	Theodore begins archiepiscopate	15
693	Willibrord's mission to Frisia	20
793	Vikings sack Lindisfarne	21
848	Birth of Alfred the Great	22
1016	Cnut rules England	25
1066	Norman conquest of England	26
1073	Gregory VII (Hildebrand) begins pontificate	31
1085	Domesday Book	35
1170	Murder of Thomas Becket	41
1208	Papal interdict of England	42
1215	Magna Carta	43
1309	Beginning of Avignon papacy	48
1348	The Black Death	49
1380	Wat Tyler's rebellion	51
1380	John Wyclif *floruit*	51
1409	Council of Pisa	66

Date		Page
1414	Council of Florence	66
1431–49	Council of Basel	66
c. 1466–1536	Erasmus	67
1484–1531	Zwingli	70
1509–64	John Calvin	70
1509	Accession of Henry VIII	75
1517	Luther's 95 theses	69
1530	Fall of Cardinal Wolsey	77
1533	Cranmer becomes Archbishop	79
1534	Succession act, repudiating papal supremacy in England	79
1538	Tyndale's Bible	80
1549	First Prayer Book of Edward VI	86
1549	Ket's rebellion	88
1552	Second Prayer Book of Edward VI	87
1553	Accession of Queen Mary	91
1558	Accession of Elizabeth I	97
1554–1600	Richard Hooker	110
1570	Bull *Regnans in Excelsis*	101
1603	Accession of James I	115
1604	Hampton Court Conference	116
1605	Gunpowder Plot	118
1607	Jamestown colony	163
1611	Authorized Version of the Bible	117
1620	Plymouth colony	163
1625	Accession of Charles I	122
1638	Scottish National Covenant	125
1640	Convocation of Long Parliament	126
1649	Execution of Charles I	127
1649	Beginning of English Commonwealth	138
1658	Death of Oliver Cromwell	141
1660	Restoration of the monarchy	141
1661	Savoy Conference	142
1662	Revision of Prayer Book	142
1678	The "Popish Plot"	145
1685	Accession of James II	145

Date		Page
1688	The "Glorious Revolution"	145
1689	Accession of William and Mary	146
1632–1704	John Locke	148
1657–1737	William Wake	210
1692–1752	Joseph Butler	151
1686–1761	William Law	152
1698	Founding of The Society for Promoting Christian Knowledge	153
1703–91	John Wesley	156
1738	Wesley's "Aldersgate Experience"	156
1759–1836	Charles Simeon	158
1729–96	Samuel Seabury	166
1785	Philadelphia General Convention	167
1789	Inauguration of American Church	169
1792–1866	John Keble	177
1800–82	Edward Bouverie Pusey	180
1801–90	John Henry Newman	179
1835–93	Phillips Brooks	196
1841	Tract 90	182
1854	Re-activation of Convocation	186
1859	Darwin's *Origin of Species*	190
1867	First Lambeth Conference	207
1888	Lambeth Quadrilateral	213
1889	*Lux Mundi*	191
1896	Bull *Apostolicae Curae*	211
1912	Consecration of V. S. Azariah	206
1931	Bonn Agreement	212
1954	First Anglican Congress	207
1967	Seattle General Convention	200

Chapter One

Dawn

And did those feet in ancient time
   Walk upon England's mountain green?
And was the holy Lamb of God
   On England's pleasant pastures seen?

And did the Countenance Divine
   Shine upon our clouded hills?
And was Jerusalem builded here
   Among those dark Satanic mills?
              William Blake

Americans tend to think that the Britain they know has been there forever. But the British are among the younger peoples in history when compared to the Chinese, the Jews, the Greeks, even the French. Civilized men of the Graeco-Roman millennium knew and cared little about Britain, since it held no advanced culture or strong military power or prime economic treasure. Its inhabitants were primitive and poor.

Moreover, the Britons of pre-Roman and Roman times were not "Englishmen" at all, but Celts. It is the present-day Irishman or Welshman or Scot, rather than the Englishman, who can trace his ethnic ancestry back to pre-Roman times. (Isn't it a well known saying that every Irishman is descended from the ancient Irish kings?) Celtic art shows a strong flair for the fantastic, marked by imaginative pas-

1

sion, a quality which expresses itself in religion as mystical ardor and vision of things unseen. One can find this quality and character in Irish and Welsh and Scottish religion without looking very hard. The Englishman's religion tends to differ in emotional intensity.* His faith may be deep and his commitment earnest, but it often seems to his Celtic neighbors that his ruling passion in religion is dispassion.

These spiritual differences, such as they are, have their foundation in ancient history. The English people come from very different forebears than do their neighbors in Britain. The Celts were there first.

Romanization

In 55 B.C. Julius Caesar conquered Britain (though not those parts of it now known as Ireland and Scotland), and claimed it for Rome. The full Roman takeover, however, came a century later. During that century, the New Creation began in another Roman province. Jesus of Nazareth lived, and suffered under Pontius Pilate. Shortly thereafter His friends were telling the world that He was alive and was Lord of all creation. In Britain, a few hundred miles away, there was no knowledge of these things. There the big concern was the determination of the emperor Claudius to subjugate Britain completely to the Roman yoke, which he did, with considerable difficulty, around the middle of the first century.

Thus began the Roman era in Britain. It was to last for almost three centuries and would be one of Britain's happiest eras. During that age, notes Churchill, "well-to-do persons in Britain lived better than they ever did until late Victorian times. From the year 400 till the year 1900 no one had central heating and very few had baths. A wealthy British-Roman citizen building a country house regarded

* Author's Note. These are tendencies we are thinking about and not fixed and rigid patterns.

the hypocaust which warmed it as indispensable. For fifteen hundred years his descendants lived in the cold of unheated dwellings, mitigated by occasional roastings of gigantic wasteful fires."[1] A time of troubles would follow the Roman age during which Britains would remember with longing the peace, order, security, and comfort of *Romanitas*. Rome had become deeply and permanently associated in the British mind with ordered peace and justice under law, a fact which would function vitally in the shaping of British Christianity in the ages to come.

The coming of Christianity

Who first brought the Gospel to Britain, and when, is unknown. Legends, some of them admirably specific, are numerous, but the verifiable facts are few. Among these legends is the most charming one that tells how St. Joseph of Arimathea came to Britain and planted the Glastonbury Thorn, but this is a medieval tale. We know there were Christians in Britain early in the third century, and there must have been some well before this; but how many, and where they were, and what their cultus was like in detail, are unanswerable questions. The legalization of Christianity throughout the Empire in 312 was followed by a tremendous advance of the faith everywhere, but our evidence for this period in Britain is negligible. This is most probably because the British Christians were poor and obscure folk who left no monuments or records and whom history does not remember.

One illustrious name does remain to us, however, from this dark age. It is that of St. Alban, the first (known) British martyr. He is believed to have died in the persecution ordered by Diocletian *c*. 305. Alban was a pagan who sheltered a fugitive priest, and was converted and baptized by this priest. The story[2] has it that when soldiers traced the fugitive to Alban's house, Alban donned the priest's clothing and let himself be taken, condemned, and put to death. Alban has always held a high place in the British roll of saints and martyrs.

Pelagius

Because Roman Britain has the dubious honor of being the homeland of the heretic Pelagius, and because the Pelagian controversy was important in the development of Christian doctrine, we take note here of the man and the movement that bears his name. Pelagius was probably a Romanized Celt, and possibly an Irishman. As a lay monk he went to Rome in about 400 to study, and he did most of his preaching and teaching in the Mediterranean area rather than in Britain. Nevertheless his teachings drew a following at home. He had read the writings of St. Augustine of Hippo in which the African doctor set forth his doctrine of the depravity of man resulting from the Fall. This doctrine seemed to Pelagius to degrade human nature, and also to dishonor God by implying that Jesus would set before His followers a way of life and salvation which, on Augustine's theory of human depravity, man was incapable by his own choice of embracing and following. According to Augustine, a man's even wanting to be good is itself a work of divine grace, while according to Pelagius, it is up to man both to choose the good and to do it "on his own," because God has made man capable of this.

The heresy of Pelagianism consists in the belief that man attains salvation by his own virtuous choice and effort rather than by God's grace.

The Pelagian teaching in Britain drew a strong enough following to disturb the orthodox, who appealed to the Church in Gaul for help in combating it. Their appeal brought to Britain St. Germanus, Bishop of Auxerre, in 429, to lead the orthodox assault upon Pelagianism.

We often hear it suggested that there is a specially strong taint of Pelagianism in the very blood of Anglo-Saxons, so that Englishmen and also Americans are peculiarly afflicted by it. It does seem that England and America rather abound in "do-it-yourself religion" of one kind or another. But as a matter of definite doctrine Pelagianism is rejected by Anglicanism no less than by Roman Catholicism, Lutheranism and Calvinism. The truth is that there is an element of unconscious Pelagianism in any man who imagines that he "stands on his own feet" morally. It is an optimistic doctrine of man, and therefore to be found wherever man thinks well of himself—which is everywhere.

Ireland

The patron saint of Ireland and the planter of the faith there was not an Irishman but a pre-English Briton, born about 389. His father was a Roman citizen and a Christian deacon. As a boy of 16, Patrick was captured by raiders and sold into slavery in Ireland. A few years later he escaped to Gaul, where he was sheltered and educated by monks. He longed to return to Ireland as an apostle of Christ, having an extraordinary love and concern for the land of his bondage. St. Palladius had already established a mission in Ireland which was having little success. It seems that druidism, the traditional Celtic cult, was making a powerful last stand in Ireland, against the powerfully advancing force of Christianity.

Patrick was sent to assist Palladius, and he brought to the mission the fire and life it needed. He was consecrated a bishop in 432, and his work during the next thirty years was that of an apostolic genius. The result of it was a quite thoroughly Christianized Ireland which, unlike the larger island to the east, would never lapse into paganism. A time would come when a heathenized Britain would have to be re-evangelized largely by Irish monks.

Scotland

Before the end of the fourth century there were Christian missionaries at work in Scotland. The best known of these was St. Ninian (c. 360–c. 432). Born of Cumbrian British stock, he went to Rome in his youth to be instructed in the faith. In 394 he was consecrated a bishop in Rome and sent out to convert Scotland. His work, though heroic, fell far short of that goal.

The complete conversion of Scotland belongs to the sixth century, and was the result of the work of St. Columba (521–597) and his companions who came from Ireland to found a community on the island of Iona. This community became both a base of operations for missionary outreach to surrounding tribes and a center of devotion and learning. The Church of Scotland was born in Iona, and St. Columba more than any other deserves to be called its father founder.

The heathen terror

While Christianity was advancing and flourishing in Ireland in the first half of the fifth century, the Church in Britain was being routed and ruined by the invading Angles, Saxons and Jutes. Most of the Britons who escaped the sword fled westward and found refuge in Wales and Cornwall. For a century and a half Christianity became almost extinct in Britain, and was replaced by the Teutonic heathenism of the conquerors. These invading heathen were the primary progenitors of the English people, and they were Germans, not Celts or Gauls. They brought with them their ancestral religion. Their heroic gods dwelling and feasting in Valhalla were gusty giants who gave victory to brave warriors here below, and at last a rousing welcome to the everlasting banquet of gods and brave men above. As primitive folk religions go, this one was by no means a bad one. The old heathenism was a spent force, however. It could not resist the challenge of the new Christian faith for long when directly confronted by it.

Another spent force in this age of change was *Romanitas*. The mighty Empire was crumbling and tottering. Historians have long pondered the reasons for its decline and fall, and there is no solid scholarly consensus on the point to this day. One of the moot questions is whether Christianity contributed to the decline of Rome, or whether the decline of Rome made the triumph of Christianity possible. We may leave the question as we found it. What is germane for us is that the Empire was powerless to prevent the Teutonic tribes from overrunning Roman Britain. The legions had been withdrawn, one by one, from such outposts as Britain to defend the shrinking frontiers.

If the British Christians supposed, as we may be sure they did, that the Peace of Christ and the *Pax Romana* were somehow bound up with each other, they were now cruelly educated into the truth that Christ's peace is not as this world gives. Left helpless as sheep beset by wolves, they learned through terrible tribulation that the Sign of the Cross is not a good luck charm.

[1] Winston Churchill, A *History of the English Speaking Peoples*, I, 35.
[2] Bede, *Ecclesiastical History of the English People*, i.7.

Chapter Two

Celt, Saxon and Roman

No race took over Christianity with so much originality as did the Celts.

Ernest Renan

In Ireland Christianity became Irish and Celtic, which means that it became mystical, individualistic, imaginative, and passionate. As soon as it took definite form it was something very different from anything on the continent. To be sure, its creed was that of all western Christendom, and it was strongly monastic, as was the Church everywhere else. But it was not territorially organized under diocesan bishops. The basic unit of the Irish Church was the small monastic group, ruled by the abbot, who may or may not have been a bishop. How the Irish Church came by its peculiarities can only be guessed at. Some scholars have held that some features of the Irish Church were a development from the colleges of Druids which the Church replaced. More plausible is the theory that the formation of the Christian community was shaped by the Celtic tribal order. Whatever the explanation, Irish Christianity manifested an extraordinary originality, as Renan observed.

The Irish monks of the fifth and sixth centuries showed three grand passions: for study, for severe eremitic asceti-

cism, and for travel. This combination made them bold and
zealous missionaries. Seafaring Irish monks may have visited
Iceland two full centuries before the Northmen arrived
there.[1]

To the Irish Church far more than to any other institution we owe the preservation of what we have of the classic
Greek and Roman literatures. The old Roman schools had
been destroyed by the barbarians. Most Christians abhorred
the pagan classics as unfit for Christian consumption. The
Irish, and later the Anglo-Saxons, did not share this preju-
dice, and kept the classical tradition alive.

Wales

The Church in Wales was the remnant of the Romano-
British Church after the Anglo-Saxons had driven it from
most of the land. The patron saint of Wales, St. David,
lived through most of the sixth century and accomplished
much in the strengthening and deepening of the faith of
his people. He was a typically extreme Celtic ascetic, given
to such penances as standing frozen in cold water.

This Celtic Christianity of the sixth century was in most
ways superior to the religion of the British Church which
the Anglo-Saxons had destroyed. After the terrible blows
from the heathen hammer the refugees had regrouped themselves, and, in their affliction, were born again into a new
character. They became adventurous, crusading and zealous.
Their religion lacked only one necessary element: a love for
their enemies and conquerors. They were willing to leave
the heathen Anglo-Saxons to perdition, and here began the
separation between Celt and Anglo-Saxon which has un-
happily persisted through the ages. When Augustine came
from Rome near the end of the sixth century to evangelize
the English he looked to the Welsh Christians for help and

did not get it. Their refusal meant that the Anglo-Saxons would be evangelized primarily by Roman Christians.

The Roman mission

The next important chapter in British Christian history begins in the heart and prayers of St. Gregory the Great, who became pope in 590. According to a beautiful story,[2] which may well be true, Gregory while a young man in Rome saw some fair-skinned boys for sale in the slave market, and was told that they were Angles. "Not Angles but angels," he remarked. He set his heart upon bringing the faraway British heathen into Christ's fold, and when he became pope he established a mission under the leadership of Augustine (not to be confused with the bishop and theologian Augustine of Hippo). Augustine was a true Roman and a true soldier of Christ—a man under authority; but he lacked Gregory's graciousness and humility.

Augustine and his party reached Kent early in 597. In a very short time the Kentish king Ethelbert and most of his court had been baptized, and the whole nation of Kent followed. Later that year Augustine was consecrated a bishop.

The following year Augustine submitted some questions to the pope concerning liturgy and church order. There was then no uniform liturgical usage throughout Christendom, and Augustine wanted to know what he was to do in Britain about the several different ways of celebrating the eucharist. The pope's reply was that he was to take whatever he had found good anywhere in the Church and make this the custom in Britain. Some nine centuries later, Thomas Cranmer, compiler of the Book of Common Prayer, would carry out his task of liturgical reform with much the same mind as was in Pope Gregory I.

Augustine met with stiff resistance from the British clergy who were already there when he came. His demands do not strike us as excessive. They were to keep Easter at the Roman time, to baptize in the Roman way, to join with him in the mission to the Anglo-Saxons, and to recognize his authority over them. For several reasons they resisted. One reason was his overbearing manner. Another was their hatred for the Anglo-Saxons. Above all, there was their love for their own Celtic customs and ways. They feared that to surrender a little of their inheritance would be in the end to lose all. As Augustine wrestled with these obstacles he lost his temper and made a terrible prediction: that if the Celts would not bring life to the English, the English would bring death to the Celts. His prediction would be remembered with a shudder after the battle of Chester in 615, in which many British clergy fell.

One of Augustine's associates, Paulinus, was made a bishop in 625 to head a mission to Northumbria. The baptism of the Northumbrian king Edwin in 627 was another of those momentous royal baptisms signalling the "conversion" of a nation. The success of the Northumbrian mission was amazingly rapid but also amazingly short-lived. After Edwin's death there was a revival of heathenism which almost obliterated Christianity. This kind of sudden collapse of Christianity in that age was quite common, largely because such "conversions" of whole people by royal example or command were only skin-deep. Under Edwin's nephew, Oswald, Christianity rallied and revived. The king was aided by a task force of monks from Iona led by St. Aidan. Few more fruitful partnerships are to be found anywhere in history than this one of Oswald and Aidan. Thus Northumbria was evangelized, and later re-evangelized, by Scottish monks trained in the Celtic tradition.

That part of England known as the Midlands remained longest in heathenism. Its conversion in the seventh century was the work of Irish monks who looked to Lindisfarne as their spiritual home; so here, too, we see a Celtic mission— not Roman.

Whitby

As Christianity spread and took root in England it became clear that the English must make a definite choice
between the Roman and the Celtic ways. The issue came to
a head in 664 when Oswy, King of Northumbria, who followed the Celtic calendar, realized that he would be keeping Easter several weeks before his wife, who followed the
Roman. He felt that a choice for one way or the other had
to be made, and summoned a council to meet at Whitby in
the fall of that year. Oswy presided, and the Celts and
Romans were equally represented. Colman, speaking for the
Celtic cause, defended the Celtic Easter date by claiming
for it the authority of St. John. Wilfrid, pleading the Roman
case, claimed the authority of St. Peter. Wilfrid won the
case; Oswy decided for the Roman cause.

This decision did much more than settle the controversy
about the Easter date. It settled the future of English Christianity. Henceforth the English Church would be a fully
functioning part of the Church of which the Bishop of
Rome was the ruling head. Henceforth Rome, not Iona or
Lindisfarne, would rule the English Church. It would be a
relatively loose and remote control, since Rome was far from
Britain and communication was slow and difficult. Nevertheless, as a result of the decision at Whitby, the papal rule
became normal and accepted; faith and worship became
more uniform, and more like what was to be found on the
continent; and monasticism became more moderate, less
austere.

In considering this transition from the Celtic to the
Roman orders it should not be supposed that all Celtic
Christian leaders were simply dead set against Rome. So
characteristically Celtic a man as St. Cuthbert, Bishop of
Lindisfarne, for example, evidently supported the move-
ment toward Rome because he felt that it was the right

course for the British Church to follow into the future. There must have been others of the same mind, since we know that some Celts went to Rome for their education.

Celtic summary

The Celtic Church was orthodox in all fundamentals of the faith. Its liturgy was thoroughly catholic, albeit distinct and different from the major uses on the continent. The eucharist was central, celebrated on Sundays and holy days with mixed chalice, unleavened bread, and communion in both kinds. The sacrifice of the mass, and the real presence of Christ in the sacrament, were taught. Ordination was always conferred by a bishop, although the rule requiring the joint participation of three bishops in the consecration of a bishop was not always followed. This irregularity led to some doubt in the English Church about the validity of Celtic orders.

Confession, both public, and private, had a prominent place in Celtic religion. One's confessor was known as a "soul-friend" and gave spiritual direction as well as absolution. What came to be the penitential code of the whole Western Church may well have originated in Ireland, from which it began spreading in the seventh century to England and throughout the continent.

[1] For this and other pertinent facts see John Godfrey, *The Church of Anglo-Saxon England*, 38. Cambridge.
[2] Bede, *Ecclesiastical History of the English Nation*, II.1.

Chapter Three

A Century of Planting

The violence of northern savages exasperated Christianity into power. It lived by the love of the people. Bishop Wilfrid manumitted two hundred and fifty serfs, whom he found attached to the soil. The clergy obtained respite from labor for the boor on the Sabbath, and on church festivals. "The lord who compelled his boor to labor between sunset on Saturday and sunset on Sunday, forfeited him altogether." The priest came out of the people, and sympathized with his class. The church was the mediator, check, and democratic principle, in Europe.

Ralph Waldo Emerson

Theodore of Tarsus was the first Archbishop of Canterbury to be appointed by a pope and the first, as Bede noted, whom the whole nation obeyed.[1] He was himself neither a Roman nor an Englishman but a native of Cilicia, St. Paul's native province, where he was born about 602. He was well educated in Greek philosophy at Athens before coming to Rome, where his abilities were recognized by the Church's leaders. We can only guess why Pope Vitalian chose this man for the English post; he must have been sure that Theodore, although an eastern Christian and a man of 66 years who had never been to England, was none the less the right man for the job. The pope sent along with him to Canterbury two extra-ordinary assistants, Hadrian a North

African and Benedict Biscop a Northumbrian, both of whom were ardent Romanophiles.

When they arrived in England in 669 they found a very sick church, despite the fact that England had been Christian, off and on, for three centuries. The mass conversions had been superficial. There had not been an effective settled pastoral ministry to keep the people growing in the faith. The clergy were commonly ignorant and morally lax. The Roman mission begun by Gregory had not been sustained. Just before the coming of Theodore a terrible plague had swept over the land. The whole picture was gloomy and the prospect dark as Theodore began his task of massive reconstruction of the English Church, a task which would occupy him for more than twenty years until he died at 88.

His accomplishments were manifold. He brought the English Church into full working union with the Roman Church, and overhauled the ecclesiastical structure so as to provide episcopal and pastoral care for all the people. He raised the intellectual and moral standards of the clergy, and he did this with the native, *i.e.* Anglo-Saxon, clergy rather than by importing men from abroad. Though he came from Rome appointed by the pope, he made and kept the English Church most thoroughly English. At the same time, during Theodore's time it became common for Englishmen to make pilgrimages to Rome, and it is certain that as they returned home from the eternal city, so rich in apostolic tradition, they strengthened in England the growing bond with Rome.

Theodore himself was eminent as a physician of souls, and after his death a collation of his moral judgments was made under the title of the *Penitentiale*. The English Church's special concern for moral theology probably begins with this. He had learned from the Celtic moral theology something he thought most valuable: the art of using penances remedially, to help with the healing of the sinner. A thousand years later, the Anglican Jeremy Taylor would make this concept the basis of his spiritual direction.

Wilfrid

We have noted that the successful pleader of the Roman cause at the Council of Whitby was Wilfrid. A younger contemporary of Theodore who gave the Archbishop no end of trouble, he must none the less be credited with having done much to integrate the English Church into the Roman order and system. Born in 634 of a noble Northumbrian family, Wilfrid left home at 14, eager, as his biographer put it, for the kingdom of heaven. He never lost that celestial appetite, which was undoubtedly genuine. But he had another appetite along with it, this one for worldly power and pomp.

Because the man was very complex so was his career, and to attempt to relate it in detail would only be confusing. He was Bishop of York, but spent much of his time in exile resulting from his quarrels with the Northumbrian king and with his ecclesiastical peers. His lasting importance in English Church history lies in several facts. He was a zealous missionary and through both accomplishment and example did much to make English Christians aware of their mission to the heathen world. He, perhaps even more than Theodore, Romanized the Church in such areas as doctrine, worship, and order. In his own person and performance he introduced to the English the idea that a lowly Christian "servant of the servants of God" may, and should, seek wealth and worldly power for the sake of serving Christ most effectively. Whether this was ultimately for the blessing or the bane of God's people only God can judge. Finally, Wilfrid started something which was to become a momentous precedent when he appealed to the pope for help and support in his political and ecclesiastical conflict at home. Such appeals to Rome by embattled English Churchmen in later times would become a major issue between Rome and England.

Church life

England was missionary territory when Theodore arrived in 669. Within a century, the whole land was Christian.

This century saw the birth of the parish system, consisting of a local church with a resident pastor. The parish was born as part of the developing manorial system. The thane who ruled the manor built his own church, maintained it, and claimed the right to appoint its pastor. The parish priest was his lord's man in the feudal sense, subject to his lord's authority, but he was not a serf. He was given a portion of the manorial land, called the glebe, and he lived by its produce. He had to be nominated by his lay patron, but only the bishop could institute and induct him. The parish priest had certain dues from his people as well as the glebe. Chief of these church taxes was the tithe, consisting of one-tenth of all the produce of land and livestock. The tithe began as a voluntary offering. Later the Church undertook to make it compulsory, and finally succeeded, but only after three hundred years of hard struggle.

The Celtic Church had been dominated by a monasticism which was austerely ascetic and individualistic, centred in the holy man who was a hermit rather than the community of brethren living comparatively "in the world." There had developed on the continent the communal monasticism of the kind associated with the Rule of St. Benedict. Wilfrid introduced this rule into England and it soon prevailed, with powerful and manifold effect not only upon the life of the Religious themselves but upon the life of the whole community.

Benedict Biscop, who came to England with Theodore, did much to promote monastic education, but in this age education began to flourish outside the monasteries as well. Theodore and Hadrian, who taught at Canterbury, went beyond the range of strictly ecclesiastical studies and offered instruction in such fields as Greek, classical Latin, astronomy, arithmetic and medicine. It was the beginning of the union of religion and learning in England.

The scholars

Under the impetus provided by Theodore and Hadrian, English scholarship flourished and became known throughout Europe. The first eminent figure is Aldhelm (c. 639–709). A child of the royal house of Wessex, he was sent to Ireland to study under the famous teacher Maildubh, but he transferred to Canterbury to complete his education under Theodore and Hadrian. He became a polymath, expert in such fields as Roman law, poetry, astronomy and mathematics; but withal he remained a simple, holy man of God.

The next of England's famous scholars is known as the Venerable Bede. He was born in northern England in 673. His fame rests upon his *Ecclesiastical History of the English People*, without which one cannot study English history. Bede was raised from childhood by Benedict Biscop at Jarrow and there he spent his whole life of some sixty years. Although his enduring fame rests upon his history, he was known throughout Europe as a theologian, a biblical scholar who had mastered Hebrew and Greek, a scientist, and a poet.

The third illustrious scholar is Alcuin, born c. 730 of a noble Northumbrian family. Historians credit him with being the inspirer of the Carolingian renaissance on the continent, because of his influence as Charlemagne's close friend, counselor and educational minister. His strongest influence was in liturgical development. The emperor Charlemagne regarded the prevailing variety of liturgical usage as inimical to good order in the Church, and so Alcuin, at his behest, made certain adaptations and changes in the eucharistic liturgy which came to be generally accepted

throughout the Frankish kingdom and eventually throughout Latin Christendom.

Literature

As English poets turned from heathen to Christian
themes the Bible became their arsenal of subject matter.
The first two famous names are Caedmon and Cynewulf.
We know Caedmon only through Bede's story of his inspiration.[2] An angel appeared in a dream to this lowly monk
and asked him to sing. The monk protested his muteness
but the angel persisted and Caedmon tried to sing. In the
morning he recalled his song and went on from there to turn
much of the Bible into verse—"put together," Bede says,
"with very great sweetness and pricking of the heart." As
England's first popular poet, Caedmon started something
that would play a large part in English religion from that
day to this—religious poetry.

Cynewulf made Christian dogma the theme of his lay.
His *Dream of the Rood* is an allegory in which the Cross is
personified and speaks to the dreaming poet, telling him the
story of the crucifixion. When he awakens he feels lonely
and forsaken, and prays to the Cross to hasten the day when
he will be raised to eternal glory with the saints.

Beowulf, the most famous of the Anglo-Saxon poems,
belongs to the seventh or eighth century. It is interesting as
a heathen folk epic, but of no direct importance to the development of specifically Christian literature. It is pagan in
substance, and the passages in it expressing Christian belief
are probably pious interpolations by Christian editors.

Overseas missions

As soon as Anglo-Saxon England found itself Christian it
became concerned about the heathen abroad. The pagan
peoples of northern Europe were their close kin. Frisia and

Saxony had held out stubbornly against Christianity. In 693 the pope established a Frisian mission under Willibrord, an Englishman. This work was carried much further in the next generation by another Englishman, Boniface, who was pre-eminently the apostle to Germany.

It is strongly possible that the English mission to Germany weakened the English Church at home by drawing off into this overseas enterprise many of its ablest sons. Whatever the cause, there was a general decline of piety as the eighth century waned. In the letters of Boniface and other sources we read depressing testimony that some bishops and clergy were falling into greed, drunkenness, and sensuality; that some kings were expropriating church lands; and that English women on pilgrimage to Rome were prostituting themselves for money to pay their way. This is the kind of thing that stern reformers like Boniface see lurking behind every bush. But it is clear that English Christianity, after its first fine rapture, was making friends with the world and the flesh. There was weakness within; and the Viking terror from without was soon to strike.

[1] *Eccl. Hist.* iv.2.
[2] *Ibid* iv.24.

Chapter Four

The Vikings

A persecutione paganorum et omnium inimicorum nostrorum,
Libera nos, Domine!
                    Anglo-Saxon litany (9th/10th century)

All the familiar legends about the Vikings are true: their
daring, their skill in war and on sea, their hardihood, their
cruelty. To the English and the Irish they seemed utter
savages, though the English and Irish themselves were not
over-civilized. What made the difference, which was wide
and deep, was only one thing: the English and Irish were
Christians, the Vikings were not, and it made the difference
between the civilized man and the savage.

The Viking age may be dated from the sacking of Lindisfarne on a winter day in 793. Lindisfarne represented Christianity, civilization, and learning, and it was destroyed by
Danish raiders with total and unmitigated ferocity. Some
monks were killed, others were carried off to the slave mar-
kets, along with a rich haul of gold, jewels, and precious
sacred vessels. The disaster sent a shudder through northern
Europe. In 802 Iona suffered the same fate. The Viking
raids, at first sporadic, developed into full-scale invasions for
possession of the land.

21

Alfred the Great

All of England would have fallen to the heathen but for
one man: Alfred, King of Wessex (848–899). In English
folk-lore Alfred stands forth as the godly king *par excellence*
and in the 15th century the pious King Henry VI petitioned
Pope Eugenius IV to canonize him.

His father, King Ethelwulf, had been a devout Christian
and Alfred was deeply religious from infancy. All his life he
was physically frail, but this did not prevent him from becoming a superb military commander. He inflicted some
stunning blows upon the superior Danish forces, but the
limits of his military achievement should be noted. The
Dane was not driven from England; the Dane was there to
stay. What Alfred did was to fight the Danes to something
of a deadlock, and to preserve Christianity. As one historian
remarks, Alfred demonstrated that the Dane could be not
only beaten but baptized. As the Norsemen settled down
in the land, their conversion to Christianity became a steady
flow.

Alfred is renowned also for his arts of peace. He carried
on a vastly ambitious program for the revival of learning in
his war-torn land. He believed in education for the layman
as for the cleric, and was one of the prophets and pioneers
of lay education in England. He stands among the most influential Christian lawgivers. Alfred's laws, amplified and
modified by his successors, provided the foundation of the
English common law. His code was based upon the Old
Testament laws superimposed upon the unwritten Anglo-
Saxon custom, all of this being adapted to conform to Chris-
tion compassion. The humane concern expressed in his laws
earned for Alfred the honorific "Protector of the poor."

The monastic revival

The Viking wars almost totally destroyed the monastic
life, and Alfred's effort to restore it in his day could not

succeed. A full century of general recovery was needed before this could be done. The monastic revival owed much to
the leadership of St. Dunstan (born c. 909), who eventually
became Archbishop of Canterbury. He did his great work
as Abbot of Glastonbury, to which place many scholars and
musicians were drawn to sit at his feet. These men went out
imbued with Dunstan's principles to found new monastic
houses. Through his influence the Rule of St. Benedict was
established as the norm throughout England, with some
adaptations to English custom and climate. These included
a provision for prayers for the king to be offered at every
service, a practice which would become a familiar feature of
modern Anglicanism.

Overseas missions

At a time when Scandinavian marauders were ravaging
England, English Churchmen were carrying the Gospel to
Scandinavian lands. Many of these missionaries presumably
were themselves Danes or Norwegians who had spent some
time in England or Ireland, had become Christians while
there, and then had returned to their homelands as ardent
missionaries of Christ. Their enterprise of faith and love
proved most fruitful, for both Denmark and Norway were
substantially won to Christianity in the tenth century—
solidly and permanently. I say "substantially won"; by this
I mean that the seed of the Gospel had been securely sown.
But there is much evidence that once these Scandinavian
peoples were baptized the process of their becoming consistently Christian in their thinking and living was only
begun, and commonly took not several years but several
generations. Even so, the light of faith which finally scattered the darkness of the old Nordic paganism was carried
from lamps in England and Ireland, and we have noted
how at an earlier time the Englishman Boniface became the
apostle to Germany.

The millennial year

Throughout Europe in many regions the approach of the year 1000 A.D. filled many Christian hearts with foreboding, as they wondered if Christ would come to earth in his last judgment. For some reason this chiliastic panic did not affect the English on any large scale, if at all. The state of the Church in England in the millennial year was good, and promising.

There were many new monastic houses, and the best kind of men and women were entering the cloisters.

There were now 18 dioceses in England, and so many clergy and parishes in some of them that the archdeacon, as an administrative aide to the diocesan bishop, had to be invented.*

The parish clergy were mostly local men of little education but of generally good character. Most of the secular priests married, but in the second half of the tenth century reformers were putting pressure on married candidates for holy orders to put away their wives at ordination and to vow celibacy. However, as the Church moved into the 11th century this reform had made little headway in England.

The lay people attended church regularly, were faithful in the sacraments, and saw their Christian duty to live sober and godly lives. Nevertheless, heathen practices and many superstitions remained and there had to be church laws forbidding such things as the worship of fountains, necromancy, and enchantments.

Royal politics

Two groups of Danes in England should be clearly distinguished: those who came only to plunder, then to go back

* Author's Note. England has not always rejoiced in this invention.

home, and those who settled down in England to become Englishmen. The result was that there was a Danish nation as a whole, or people, which really occupied two lands— Denmark and England; and regardless of where they lived they retained their sense of Danish national identity. There was not yet a single English nation by any means. The process of national unification had begun under Alfred, but as the 11th century opened it was far from complete.

In 1016 the Danish Cnut made himself master and king of England, being acknowledged as such by most of the English magnates. He had won his position against valiant Anglo-Saxon resistance and he tried to conciliate English feeling in every way possible. A Christian by conversion and deep conviction, he became one of England's best kings. He dreamed of making the North Sea an Anglo-Danish lake, with England heading a Nordic confederation stretching from Ireland to the Baltic, but this dream died with him, in 1035.

Eight years later, the British monarchy was restored with the crowning of Edward, whose mother, Emma, was sister of Count Robert of Normandy, and whose father, Ethelred, was a direct descendant of Alfred the Great. After Ethelred's death Cnut had married Emma. The leader of the Danish party in England, Godwin of Wessex, was the supremely strong man in the land at this juncture, and was determined to remain so. Edward was a weakling, whom Godwin was sure he could handle, and so Godwin engineered putting him on the throne. The new king was called "the Confessor" because of his piety, which was genuine but narrow. Edward had lived in Normandy from his childhood. His outlook and loyalties were Norman, not English, and he regarded his English countrymen as barbarians. He surrounded himself with Norman courtiers and filled the highest church offices with Normans. Thus there developed a Norman power elite around the throne. Edward had been forced to take as his wife one of Earl Godwin's daughters, as part of Godwin's program for making and keeping the king subservient to

him. When Godwin died in 1053 his son Harold succeeded
to his earldom and great estates. The house of Godwin
might well have become the royal house of England if his
sons had been able to stick together, but they fell apart in
dissension. An ambitious Norman duke named William,
who believed that he should be king of England, saw this
dissension and began to scheme.

At Edward's death in 1065 the Witan, or Great Council,
chose Harold son of Godwin to be king. He reigned for a
few months. But William the Norman, mentioned above,
the illegitimate son of Count Robert of Normandy, was
Edward's first cousin, and claimed that Edward had promised him the throne. He planned a conquest and made it
also a crusade by soliciting, and getting, the blessing of Pope
Alexander II upon his enterprise. He was able to persuade
the pontiff that England was rightly his, that Harold was a
usurper. Moreover, Harold had been crowned by Stigand,
Archbishop of Canterbury, who had received the pallium
from a schismatic pope. This meant that Rome could not
recognize Harold as king. There was more to William's
claim upon the papacy, however. He was reputed to be
friendly to reform in the Church, and promised that if God
gave him the crown of England he would devote himself to
reforming the Church in England. Hildebrand, the future
Pope Gregory VII, urged the pope to give his blessing to
this crusade, and the pope did. It was a boon that enormously strengthened William's position.

What happened at Hastings on October 14, 1066, is ele-
mentary schoolboy history. The Norman conquest brought
to an end an era of seven centuries of an English Christianity
which had been born in Roman Britain and had passed
successively through Celtic, Anglo-Saxon and Scandinavian
stages. From the time of Augustine's mission four centuries
earlier, the English Church had been within the papal orbit.
In the Norman era the papal rule would be greatly strengthened, although, as we shall see, William himself would not
subordinate the crown to the tiara in all matters.

Some things that had become parts of English Christianity before the Conquest remained and endured. Among these were the strong union of religion with learning; the Christianization of the common law; and zeal for evangelizing heathen.

Even so, it was the end of an era; the end of an age; the end of an insular world.

Chapter Five

Crown and Papacy

Tu regere imperio populos, Romane, memento
(Hae tibi erunt artes), pacisque imponere morem,
Parcere subjectis et debellare superbos.

See to it, Roman, that you rule the peoples under your sway, for
this is your genius and calling: to impose peace and order, to
spare the conquered, to cut down the proud.

Vergil, *Aenead*, vi. 851

Although French was their language, the Normans were
Norsemen. Rollo (Rolf) the Viking had obtained the
Duchy of Normandy in 911, where he and his fellow bucca-
neers settled down to become Christian knights, and faithful
sons of the Church. They were a titanic people in war and
in social organization. They took up Christianity with ardor,
as they did everything else; but it must be said that, generally speaking, the spirit of the Gospel, the spirit of lowly
service of God and men, eluded them. Sir Arthur Bryant
makes this perceptive observation:

Their buildings expressed their religion. Their patron-saint,
standing over their churches with up-lifted sword and out-
stretched wings, was the warrior archangel Michael, guardian of
Heaven; their conception of God a feudal overlord, ready to re-
ward those who like themselves kept the letter of His law. With
the spirit they troubled themselves little; they were a practical
folk who loved clear definitions. They built, not for comfort like

the timber-loving Saxons, but in stone to endure. Their serried arches, marching like armies through space, the vast halls and pillars supporting them, the rude, demon-haunted figures gazing down from their capitals, symbolized the crude magnificence and vigor of their half-barbaric minds. With their grim massiveness and twin-towers rising into the sky like swords, such churches seemed designed, as Henry James wrote, to force Heaven: "all of them look as though they had fought at Hastings or stormed Jerusalem."[1]

William the Conqueror

The first of England's Norman rulers made English kingship an enormously stronger institution than it had been before, and here one of history's ironies may be noted: he had gained the English throne with a pope's blessing, and he so shaped and strengthened the monarchy that one of his royal successors, Henry VIII, was able to defy another pope five centuries later.

William and the great reforming pope, Gregory VII, were contemporaries, and came to power as the first millennium of Christian history had been completed. Throughout this age the papacy had been a developing institution, growing in power but not in a steady upward line. The development had been uneven and spasmodic. These fluctuations in papal power had been felt less in England than on the continent, for simple reasons of geography. Its remoteness had forced the English Church to do its work and face its troubles with little help from Rome, so that a kind of ecclesiastical home rule had prevailed. It was not anti-papal, simply pragmatic accommodation. The English Christian before the Conquest revered the holy father in Rome. But Rome was far away, while the Viking, the devil, the plague, the unjust lord, all his other problems were near at hand; so he looked to his priest or his bishop or the abbot of the nearby monastery for spiritual counsel, blessing upon his crops, curses

upon his enemies, or any other useful clerical services he
needed.

As the Normans were taking over in England, the so-called
Cluniac or Gregorian reform of the Church was cresting on
the continent. This movement, named for the monastery of
Cluny in Burgundy where it began, aimed at radical reform
of the Church from the papacy on downward and outward.
The reformers saw the world as very evil, but they saw it also
as being in the Church as well as around it, so reform had
to begin within the house of God. The first step was to trans-
form the clergy into an army of soldiers of Christ. Christ in
heaven was the supreme commander. His vicar on earth, the
pope, was vice-commander in the field to whom all soldiers
must give unquestioning obedience as to the Lord himself.
It was believed that only such a disciplined and regimented
Church could accomplish the enormous task God had given
it, of bringing all men and all human affairs under Christ's
dominion.

The program called for some specific reforms. One was
the abolition of lay control of the Church as this took the
forms of simony and lay investitures. Simony in that age
consisted of the sale of church offices and benefices by the
lords who controlled them. Lay investiture was the bestowal
of ecclesiastical title and position by a secular lord rather
than by the Church. These two abuses had to be abolished
if all clerics were to be made solely accountable to their
ecclesiastical superiors. So long as a man's benefice or position was given to him by a lay lord, the man had a divided
loyalty and a dual allegiance. Another goal of the reform
movement was the imposition of celibacy upon all clergy.
Modern students commonly mistake the purpose behind
this. It was not sexual asceticism; rather it was the fear of
a clerical caste system which could easily develop within
the feudal order, in which a father could pass on his cure of
souls to his son. The church reformers were asserting that
the bestowal of any ecclesiastical office or benefice must lie
solely with the Church in the sense of the hierarchy. On that

principle there could be no lay appointment, and there could be no transmission of church office by inheritance. Also on the side of a universal rule of clerical celibacy was the idea that an unmarried priest, being free from family cares, could be more completely usable to the Church and could give himself more unconditionally to his ministry.

Hildebrand

Hildebrand's pontificate, as Pope Gregory VII, lasted only twelve years (1073–1085), but few reigns in all papal history have had comparable consequences. Because he was able to humble the German emperor of the so-called Holy Roman Empire in a show-down struggle for power which all the world was watching, it was settled that for centuries the whole life of Europe in all its aspects, temporal as well as spiritual, would be dominated by the papacy. The Hilde-brandine principle was that God had given to the papacy not only universal but comprehensive authority, so that earthly rulers are properly subordinate and subject to the pope in *all* matters. Here was an ideal of enlightened world rulership, a vision of a world of men and nations regenerated by obedience to Christ's vicar on earth.

Church historians have given the Hildebrandine doctrine of papal rule the label "Supremacy of the Spiritual," the "Spiritual" being the clergy headed by the pope. William was expressing in his administration of both church and state in England the view of the *Respublica Christiana*, the Christian kingdom. On this view, Christ is the king of the realm, who rules through two viceroys: the king, who has charge of things secular, and the pope, in whose control are things spiritual. Each in turn has deputies and vassals under him. Church and state are not two separate entities in the *Respublica Christiana*, but two aspects of the same body politic.

Either of these two concepts of the Christian community

takes for granted a feudal order and cannot be understood
at all if considered outside the context of that order. This
is the first fact about it which the modern reader of medieval
history must fix in mind. There are other important considerations. Viewing a man like Hildebrand, or William,
from afar, it is easy to sum him all up in some simple formula
like "power drive." Because there is presumably some *libido
dominandi* in every man it may be assumed that neither the
pope nor the king was an exception. But each of them confronted a chaos in his world which cried for a moral and
spiritual revolution. Each of them saw himself, by virtue of
his position, as called and ordained of God to set it right.
Of Pope Gregory VII more especially and certainly can it
be said, on the basis of all the evidence, that he was magni-
fying his office, not himself. There can be no reasonable
doubt that in his mind and the mind of his fellow reformers
the choice between Christ and chaos was in fact the choice
between papal supremacy under Christ, and chaos.

It is equally clear, on the evidence, that King William I
of England did not accept "Supremacy of the Spiritual"
without some large qualifications.

Lanfranc

William had a strong coadjutor in his friend and counselor Lanfranc, who was consecrated Archbishop of Canterbury in 1070. He was born an Italian and rose to eminence
as a leader of monastic reform in Normandy.

As Archbishop of Canterbury he was given a free hand to
re-organize the English Church, and he did so quite thoroughly. He began by replacing Englishmen in high positions
with Normans, not out of favoritism but because they were
more in line with the reform movement, of which Lanfranc
was a determined exponent. But at the same time he showed
a respect for English custom and vested interests that must
have been surprising to his contemporaries. He refused to

go all the way with the Roman "hard line" which required all married clergy to put away their wives, and did not enforce it in England. He refused to condemn the custom of lay investiture even after it had been condemned at a papal council in 1076. And he at least tacitly supported the king in a crucial show-down when the pope demanded that William should swear fealty to the pope and he refused openly to do so. This meant, to translate the issue into non-feudal terms, that the king would not acknowledge the pope's supremacy over him and over the realm of England in things temporal as well as spiritual. The Church in England was, temporally and institutionally, a vast landed feudal estate, and the question at issue behind the pope's demand for fealty was this: Who is lord of this estate, with the right to control it—king or pope? William claimed the lordship of the English Church, as landed estate though not as spiritual community, for the English crown; and it appears that Lanfranc backed him up in this.

The royal supremacy

Against the increasing papal claims William laid down three rules. (1) No pope would be recognized in England except by the king's consent, and no letters from the pope might be received by anybody except by the king's leave. (2) No English Church synod could enact any law without the king's sanction. (3) No baron or officer of the crown might be excommunicated without the king's approval. In addition, bishops and abbots would be chosen by the king. William made only one major concession, but this would prove troublesome in later times; he allowed the separation of church courts from civil courts. Up to this time all causes, spiritual as well as secular, had been heard in the same courts, with the bishop sitting alongside the earl as judge. From now on, ecclesiastical law would be administered in church courts with either the bishop or the archdeacon pre-

siding. William granted further that no spiritual cause, *i.e.*
a case involving a violation of ecclesiastical law, should come
before a layman. Contempt of an ecclesiastical court was
made a crime punishable under civil law. The king could not
foresee that in the next century there would be an enormous
expansion of canon law throughout Latin Christendom, and
that the papal curia would become the supreme court of
appeal. This would mean that a church tribunal sitting in
Rome could control justice throughout Europe, England
included.

Either Hildebrand or William might fittingly have taken
as his motto the text from Vergil quoted at the head of this
chapter. As a Christian king, William saw his "genius and
calling" as that of imposing "peace and order" upon his
subjects, sparing the conquered and cutting down the
superbos who dared to resist his rule. Hildebrand interpreted
his "genius and calling" as pope in the same terms. What
each did, or tried to do, was fraught with grave consequences
for the future. But each was more than a strong and gifted
individual. Each was the creature as well as director of a
powerful movement in history, and the age-long tension
and conflict between these two movements—the "Supremacy of the Spiritual" and the *Respublica Christiana*—determined in large measure the course of Christian history in
England, and, in differing ways and degrees, throughout
Europe.

[1] Sir Arthur Bryant, *Makers of England*, 135.

Chapter Six

To the Great Charter

Princes are like to heavenly bodies, which cause good or evil times; and which have much veneration, but no rest.

Sir Francis Bacon

The Domesday Book, a kind of national inventory which William ordered, may be dated 1085. Magna Carta is dated 1215. A period of 130 years separates the two famous documents, and it was during this period that England slowly emerged and took shape as a single nation: a nation, that is, in the medieval rather than modern sense; a culturally unified people under one monarch. At the outset of this period there were two distinct peoples in England—the Norman aristocrats at the top, the English natives underneath. It was largely in the 12th century that the barriers were broken down, by intermarriage and other means, and the union finally effected. It was slow in coming. In 1157 the justiciar, Richard de Lucy, could still speak of "us Normans" and of protection "against the wiles of the English."

The period is marked by an unending struggle between crown and papacy for effective rule of the land. The Norman kings, and the early Plantagenets who followed them, maintained a doctrine of monarchical authority which was almost absolute. The theology of kingship and civil power is so powerful a factor in the history of English Christianity that we need to give it special attention in this survey.

It was held by the proponents of this high doctrine of kingship that the king at his coronation ceased to be a mere layman and took on a sacerdotal character, even though apparently nobody ever attributed to him priestly or episcopal sacramental powers, such as the power to confer holy orders. He was king *dei gratia,* God's vicar within his realm. There was even a solemn liturgical expression of this veneration of the monarch, an importation from Byzantium to England by way of Normandy. Under Henry I the litany *Christus vincit, Christus regnat, Christus imperat* was chanted before his majesty. Belief that to the king was given a special charisma of healing was common in England from the time of Edward the Confessor and persisted well into the 18th century when Queen Anne touched Samuel Johnson for the scrofula. Henry II persuaded Pope Alexander III in 1161 to canonize his venerable ancestor Edward the Confessor, with the result that the English king could claim a saint among his ancestors.

Yet it was implicit in Norman kingship that the king limited his power by placing himself under law. He and his people both took an oath at his coronation to mutual obligation and allegiance.

William the Conqueror saw himself as being by God's appointment temporal lord and head of the English Church. On this principle he nominated his bishops and abbots and invested them with their insignia of office in token that they held their office *from him* and from no other lord. He presided at church councils in England. As we have noted in the preceding chapter he set curbs upon the power of the pope to interfere in English affairs. And he refused to swear fealty to the pope, because to have acknowledged his vassalage in this way would have been to relinquish his own feudal overlordship of England.

The first revolutionary change under the Norman regime was the imposition of the continental type of feudalism, a much tighter and more rigid system than had developed in Anglo-Saxon England, upon the whole of society. Before the

Conquest, the English churl (ceorl) had thought of himself as a free man and had been moving toward a larger freedom. The Norman masters ground him down into abject serfdom. Whatever the blessings of the Norman "reconstruction" it must be said that it did nothing to encourage the growth of democratic institutions. No Englishman with ambition to advance in church or court could hope for any such opportunity for a long time to come. On the other side there were two immense gains. Under the Normans England was set on the road to internal unity. And through its new ruling class England was brought into an enriching cultural communion with the more advanced societies on the continent.

The feudalization of the Church had many drastic consequences, one of which was especially important and in the end disastrous. The English bishop in times past, when he conformed to type, had been a pastor and shepherd of his people, moving among them freely as one of them, being a true father-in-God. Under the new system the bishop was virtually forced to become a feudal lord whose primary business was business—the profitable administration of his portion of the ecclesiastical estate. There may well have been no alternative, under the circumstances. It can be argued that the Church had to become feudal to do its work in a feudal world, that only by thus becoming itself a part of the power-structure could the Church mold and shape society along Christian lines. But it is equally clear that when the bishop became lord and master over the flock, rather than pastor and father, the cleavage between the higher clergy and the lower masses began, and would continue to a tragic end.

Anselm

When William I died in 1087 he was succeeded by his son William Rufus, the Red King. It was a sad falling off.

Rufus cared not a snap for the Church, except as a source of
money, and he was an open blasphemer. He was a wild
spender of other people's money, and gave away fortunes
to his favorites. Early in his royal career Rufus hit upon a
very effective way of replenishing his coffers: he would leave
abbeys and bishoprics vacant, and pocket their revenues for
himself. He did this even with the See of Canterbury.

At least one good thing can be said for Rufus, namely,
that he invited and persuaded St. Anselm to become Archbishop of Canterbury, though he lived to regret it. At the
time, Anselm was Abbot of the famous monastery of Bec.
Like Lanfranc, he was an Italian. He had studied under
Lanfranc and like his teacher was devoted to the Gregorian
reform. But the two men were of different minds about the
God-given rights of crown and papacy. Lanfranc had stood
with William I in maintaining the king's lordship of the
temporalia of the Church. Anselm had absorbed the whole
Hildebrandine doctrine of absolute and comprehensive
papal sovereignty. Against Rufus and later against Henry I
he carried on his fight for the abolition of lay investiture,
refusing to consecrate bishops whom Henry had invested.
A compromise solution (which proved to be no permanent
solution at all) was put forth in the Concordat of 1107, in
which it was agreed that bishops owed fealty to the king as
their feudal lord while the king gave way on the question
of investitures.

Anselm towers among his contemporaries as a theologian.
His famous "ontological proof" of the existence of God,
according to which our ability to hold an idea of God
"proves" the reality of God's being, has fascinated—or
exasperated—the best minds from that day to the present.

In *Cur Deus Homo?* Anselm sets forth a conception of
the Atonement which modern students often criticize for
being so "feudal," which indeed it is. It stresses the outraged
majesty of God in the face of human sin and explains
Christ's sacrifice on Calvary as the needed "satisfaction."
This imagery is borrowed from feudalism, and in a post-

feudal age it is irrelevant at best and repellent at worst. But Anselm developed it to replace a much older and assuredly much darker view, namely, that the devil has certain rights over fallen man and that Christ had to give his life as a ransom to the devil.

Anselm's stature as a theologian is known to all the world, but more should be said about his work as a humanitarian reformer in a markedly inhumane age. In 1102 he promulgated a canon which effectively put an end to the slave trade in England seven hundred years before slavery throughout the British colonies was abolished by Parliament.

The continuing struggle

The compromise between crown and papacy did not spell peace for long. Under Henry II (1133–1189) the struggle for control of the land broke out again, this time over the relation of the king's court to the church courts.

Because of the familiar story of the murder in the cathedral of St. Thomas Becket, and the king's role in that popular story as the villain, Henry suffers the obloquy which should be reserved for real rogues. He was in fact one of England's better kings.

Thomas Becket was a Londoner of Norman stock. His brilliant gifts, combined with titanic ambition, raised him as a very young man to the exalted position of royal chancellor. Here he worked with the king in strengthening the crown against the barons and the bishops. But Thomas was never simply a yes-man for the king or for anybody, and when the king attacked "benefit of clergy" he found his friend Thomas suddenly and resolutely on the other side, against him. "Benefit of clergy" was a legal privilege which provided that any cleric accused of any felony, except high treason, could demand trial in an ecclesiastical rather than a civil court. Henry found this intolerable. He wanted one law for all men, and demanded that "criminous clerks" stand trial in civil courts.

Why should the Church object to this arrangement? To understand the answer we must put ourselves into that historical situation. To the Church, the question was not simply one of justice but of authority as well. This dispute about courts was only part of the struggle going on between crown and papacy, and the ultimate issue was power. Who, under God, should rule the nation: pope or king? That was the question.

To see more clearly the dramatic aspect of the conflict between Henry and Thomas one must see the sudden metamorphosis which took place in Thomas when, in the summer of 1162, he became Archbishop of Canterbury. For eight years the two men had worked together most happily, Becket in deacon's orders, which didn't get in the way of his enjoying the best things of earthly life. He lived lavishly, outdoing even the king in opulence. When the old archbishop, Theobald, died in 1161, Henry told Becket that he was the royal choice to succeed. Becket thought the king was joking, but he wasn't. Then the idea captivated Thomas. He was ordained priest one day and consecrated archbishop the next. Instantly he was a different man. The psychological explanation will always be a matter of debate, and I offer no theory of my own. What is clear is that the once worldly Becket now become an ascetic living in almost monastic seclusion at Canterbury.

The former friendship became conflict and enmity. The quarrel was touched off by a tax matter which Henry wanted settled in a civil court. Thomas was summoned to explain a minor difficulty about one of his estates. This was his pretext for throwing down the gauntlet. He defied the king, refused to listen to the civil judgment against him, and threatened to excommunicate anybody who consented to his trial. He then fled overseas and lived abroad for six years. In 1170 a truce was reached and he returned to England, but there a host of foes and a sea of troubles awaited him. He had secured from Rome the excommunications of the Archbishop of York and the Bishops of London and Salisbury. When these prelates brought their grievance to the king he lost his temper against Becket the troublemaker and in his rage he uttered a curse upon his subjects who would not avenge him of this "low-born clerk." Four knights overheard him and stupidly inferred that the king was asking for volunteers to murder Becket. That they did, in a chapel of his cathedral on December 29, 1170.

The king was horrified and was able to clear himself of all complicity in the crime, but Rome was able to impose upon him a harsh penance and heavy indemnity. Henceforth he must allow appeals to Rome and he must abandon "any customs detrimental to the Church"—which meant specifically the retention of certain juridical powers by the civil courts as against the ecclesiastical. At once the cult of St. Thomas the Martyr began to flourish in England, and in 1173, less than three years after his death, Becket was canonized. For more than three centuries the magnificent shrine erected to him at Canterbury stood as a monument, and constant reminder to all visitors, of the triumph of Church over State, until in 1538 Henry VIII ordered it destroyed and had the name of St. Thomas removed from the service-books.

The crown had suffered a disastrous defeat in its struggle with the papacy. Now no one dared to raise the question of "criminous clerks" and, incredibly, "benefit of clergy" remained in the English statutes until 1827. Appeals of court verdicts to Rome became common practice.

King John

Richard "the Lion Hearted" succeeded his father Henry

II, and though he reigned for ten years (1189–99) he played little part in church-state relations, since during his reign he lived less than seven months in England. The rest of the time he was crusading. With the accession of Richard's brother John in 1199 the conflict between crown and papacy broke out anew. John proved a disaster to the crown cause.

That John's lack of strong character was a large factor in making his career a case study in futility is unquestionable, but it should be added that he inherited some adversities which might have been too much for a strong man. The long absence of Richard from England had meant that during his reign the larger departments of government, most notably the chancery and the exchequer, had had to function independently of direct royal control. Consequently they grew increasingly autonomous and bureaucratic. John's administration had inherited heavy war debts from Richard's, and John had to levy unpopular taxes to pay for his own wars. In his military operations in France he was unsuccessful and Normandy was lost. After this the English barons were unwilling to fight on the continent, and so the king and his barons became opponents in a financial tug-of-war.

Then came John's trouble with the Church. In 1205 Canterbury fell vacant and the king nominated his friend John de Gray, Bishop of Norwich; but the monks of Canterbury had chosen another man. Both sides appealed to Rome, and Pope Innocent III chose a third party, Stephen Langton, an Englishman who had studied at Paris and had become an eminent theologian and a close friend of the pope. John forbade Langton to enter England, so the Archbishop-elect had to live abroad for six years. The king had defied a strong and resolute pope, who struck back in March 1208 by placing all England under an interdict. All churches were closed; no masses could be said, or any public worship conducted. Only baptism and burial were allowed to continue. The king accepted this nonchalantly and retaliated by confiscating all church property and pocketing all its revenues.

In 1209 the pope excommunicated him, but this too failed to bring him to his knees.

At last, in 1212, the pope came up with the right weapon. He threatened to depose John by force, by the strong hand of King Philip of France. In face of this threat John surrendered unconditionally. In 1213 he submitted the crown of England to the papacy. Seldom has history seen a surrender so abject and complete. He agreed that henceforth England would be a feudal fief of the papacy with the king paying to the pope an annual tribute of one thousand marks. It is clear that he had no intention of keeping his word and was only playing for time, to keep the crown for himself and his son. He had made this "deal," however, and when the news of it fully got home to the mind of the nation there was a bitter reaction. To many Englishmen, probably to most, the king and the pope appeared as partners in a plot against English rights, possessions and liberties. The feudal barons, who had the most to lose by such a sell-out, were most bitter and most determined to undo the harm. Stephen Langton, Archbishop of Canterbury, now came forth as a patriotic leader. He had been consecrated by the pope and was a loyal Churchman, but he could not endure the reduction of England to a mere papal vassalage. He led the barons in their effort to restore the old order, and this led to John's next great surrender—this time to the barons, when he signed Magna Carta at Runnymede in 1215.

The Great Charter

Magna Carta is celebrated as a monument of English freedom, a great emancipation proclamation, but it may be helpful to be specific. In later times many things have been read into it which are not there. These facts about the Charter must be kept in mind: (1) It is a feudal document,

framed to meet feudal problems. The barons, as feudal ten-
ants of the king, were asserting their rights against uncurbed
feudal tyranny by the king. It was a charter of freedom for
the barons—not for everybody. (2) The "freemen" mentioned in the Charter did not include the villeins, who made
up two-thirds of the populace. (3) The "commons" were
not represented at Runnymede at all.

Yet it accomplished some good ends. It checked the
growth of royal tyranny toward absolutism. In it for the first
time the rights of Englishmen under the crown were put
into writing. Henceforth the English people would think of
the governing power as being in some sense a corporately
shared power of the community as a whole rather than as
the sole prerogative of any one man, be he king or pope. The
Charter embodied principles which were capable of progressive application and interpretation. For example, its
prohibition of feudal taxes levied purely at the whim of the
king would one day be invoked, after the feudal age was
ended, as a constitutional prohibition of purely arbitrary
personal taxes.

The Charter provides for the freedom of the Church
thus: "We have granted to God, and by this our present
charter have confirmed for us and for our heirs forever, that
the Church of England shall be free and shall have its rights
untouched and its liberties uninjured." This is no guarantee
of "religious freedom" of any kind, and does not deal even
by implication with the question of whether the pope or the
king should rule the Church. What is proclaimed is the
Church's freedom from extortionate taxation by the king,
freedom to elect men of its own choice to vacant sees and
abbeys, and freedom to operate its own courts independently
of royal control.

The immediate effect of the Charter was to weaken the
papal power in England, or, more exactly, to prevent the
tremendous augmentation of papal power which John's
surrender of the crown to the papacy would have entailed.

But if the Charter curbed the papal power in England it was only for a moment. The provision that the Church should be free to choose its own bishops and abbots would provide henceforth a constitutional pretext for papal intervention in any disputed election in the English Church.

Chapter Seven

The Great Frustration

No Politick admitteth nor ever did admit the teacher into confidence; nay ev'n the Church, with hierarchy in conclave compassing to install Saint Peter in Caesar's chair, and thereby win for men the promises for which they had loved and worship'd Christ, relax'd his heavenly code to stretch her temporal rule.

Robert Bridges, *The Testament of Beauty*, iv. 259–64[1]

The decline and fall of the medieval order was a manifold process: a great frustration, a dying of a dream. Toynbee writes:

The fall of the Hildebrandine Church is as extraordinary a spectacle as its rise; for all the virtues which had carried it to its zenith seemed to change, as it sank to its nadir, into their own exact antitheses. The divine institution which had been fighting and winning a battle for spiritual freedom against material force was now infected with the very evil which it had set itself to cast out. The Holy See which had led the struggle against simony now required the clergy to pay their dues to a Roman receipt of custom for those ecclesiastical preferments which Rome herself had forbidden them to purchase from any local secular power. The Roman Curia which had been the head and front of moral and intellectual progress now turned itself into a fastness of spiritual conservatism. The ecclesiastical sovereign power now suffered itself to be deprived by its local secular underlings—the princes of the rising parochial states—of the lion's share of the product of the financial and administrative instruments which the Papacy itself had devised in order to make its authority effective. Finally, as the local prince of a Papal principality, the Sovereign Pontiff had to content himself with the paltry consolation-prize of sovereignty over one of the least of the "successor-states" of his own lost empire. Has any institution ever given so great occasion as this to the enemies of the Lord to blaspheme?[2]

Throughout the 13th century the struggle between crown and papacy for effective ruling power continued. The popes won most of the battles, but in a losing cause. English nationalism was being born, and it would eventually grow beyond papal control.

When Henry III came to the throne in 1216 as a child of nine, a regency council had to be set up. Moreover, because the country was verging on chaos, this makeshift government had to be strong and capable. The right man to engineer this was at hand in the person of the papal legate, Cardinal Guala Biachieri. He and other papal legates did much to stabilize the country, for which they deserved gratitude. But the papal taxation was growing apace, and so was the sense of grievance about it.

Most Englishmen resented especially the papal money-raising system known as "provisions." The pope needed an ever growing army of helpers to govern the Church from Rome. He might assign an English benefice, with its revenue, to a Roman bureaucrat who never set foot in England. This bureaucrat might appoint a good and faithful priest to serve as his vicar, but the system as such was offensive.

Robert Grosseteste, the strongest English Churchman of the 13th century, openly defied the system of provisions and refused to present a nephew of the pope to a canonry at Lincoln. Grosseteste represents the classic Anglican ideal of a bishop. He was a diligent scholar in not only theology but poetry, agriculture, law and medicine. He urged that the Bible be studied in Hebrew and Greek, and his constant theological appeal was to the Scriptures rather than to the

Fathers. Spiritually and intellectually he seems to belong not to the 13th century but the 17th, the age of the Caroline Divines.

In 1272 Edward I became king. He is happily remembered for his achievements in law and jurisprudence, for which he is known as the English Justinian. Though he had a strong sense of nationalism and was jealous for the rights of the crown, he was by no means hostile to the Church. Both the kings and the popes of this age were forced into a collision course by their financial exigencies. As the cost of papal government mounted so did the cost of civil government in England, especially for the prosecution of almost incessant wars in France, Wales and Scotland. Both king and pope had to squeeze every drop of revenue they could get from the people. The clergy were in a peculiarly hard position, since they owed absolute obedience to the Church while they were also English subjects. Crushed between these two millstones they grew more confused and bitter.

The 14th century

An over-all view of the 14th century in England and Europe provides a somber picture. In England the main causes of distress were the Black Death, insurrection, and crushing taxation.

It was during this century that the papacy underwent the humiliation of its "Babylonish Captivity" at Avignon. The Hildebrandine concept of papal sovereignty had reached its fullest expression in the pontificate of Innocent III (1198–1216). From this papal zenith the story is one of decline and disillusionment. The temporal claims of the papacy received one crippling blow after another, until the popes were forced to leave Rome. From 1309 to 1377 the papacy was lodged at Avignon on the Rhone and all the popes were Frenchmen. It seemed to the world that the papacy had be-

come a French institution. Since during much of this time
England and France were at war, inevitably to English eyes
the papacy appeared as an ally and tool of the national
enemy.

Another cause of anti-papal feeling in England was the
suppression of the Templars. They were laymen pledged to
defend the Holy Land and to protect pilgrims. By the 14th
century they had become the financiers of Europe. King
Philip of France coveted their wealth and feared their influence. Accusing them of abominable crimes he persecuted
them cruelly, and was able to force Pope Clement V to ap-
prove the use of torture in extracting confessions from the
accused. This pope ordered that torture be allowed in English courts in the prosecution of Templars. It may be that in
England the threat of torture was never carried into action;
but general reaction against the papal order was bitter.

In the second half of the 14th century the government
passed a series of acts to curb the papal power. But the popes
were not the only targets of this legislation. There was growing animosity against the clergy as such, especially the higher
clergy and the friars. This feeling is expressed in William
Langland's prophetic poem, *Piers the Plowman.* The poet's
cry is "England for England!" He denounces the pope for
meddling in English benefices and appointing foreigners to
them; he denounces the export of English money to Avignon or Rome, and he proposes that pious Englishmen
should make their pilgrimages, not to St. Peter's in Rome
but to jails, hospitals, and the cottages of the poor in their
own neighborhoods. There can be no doubt that Langland
expressed the feelings of a growing body of Englishmen.

The Black Death

It is hard to assess the consequences of the horror which
struck England in 1348 and in two years had killed half the

populace. Many clergy hazarded their lives faithfully, ministering to the dying and burying the dead; but there was also much cowardly evasion of duty.[3] Coulton remarks:

After all, priests and monks and nuns were men and women, and they fled no more than the doctors and notaries; sometimes even less. Yet the horrible trial did show them as men and women; and the rest of medieval history is deeply colored by the revelation, so convincing in its completeness and universality, that the priests, the class who had sometimes been quasi-deified—those who could be said in loose language to "make the body of Christ" —were almost as panic-stricken as the rest of mankind.[4]

The Black Death was one of those events of which it is said that the world can never be the same after it. Those who survived it meditated as never before upon God and his providence, his Church upon earth, and the nature—and limits—of the salvific powers which God had committed to his ministers. The common man had been led to believe that the influence of the clergy in the heavenly courts was such that they could prevent such catastrophes from happening. But the Black Death had happened. It helped to undermine general trust and confidence in the established ecclesiastical order.

The great revolt

The Black Death had created a wide-spread but aimless discontent, especially among those who had been serfs. So many had died in the plague that for once the laborer could bargain with the employer, who desperately needed his help. Many were able thus to purchase their freedom from serfdom and to become free, though poor, yeoman farmers. Having had a whiff of freedom's air these men wanted more. The government, fearing the unrest, enacted the Statute of Laborers in 1351 which tried to limit wages and to bind the worker to his present occupation. The workers would not be cowed, and they openly rebelled at the poll taxes levied in 1380 and 1381. An army of these rural rebels, led by Wat Tyler, marched on London and actually occupied the city. Among the rebels were some clergy, notably John Ball. These priests boldly denounced social and political injustices, but they were almost entirely minor clergy. For this was rebellion against the feudal system, and the Church itself was an enormously rich feudal landlord.

Wyclif and Lollardy

John Wyclif (c. 1328–84) has long been called the "Morning Star of the Reformation." Some modern historians have challenged the fitness of this title for various reasons. It can properly be said, however, that he anticipated the reformers of two centuries later in some important respects.

He was by profession a scholar and by nature a prophet and reformer. He was renowned as Oxford's most eminent theologian. His master was Augustine of Hippo, whose predestinarianism he found especially congenial. For years Wyclif's lectures aroused no serious attention, until, in 1376, lecturing on civil lordship, he attacked the wealth of the Church and the interference of popes and high clerics in civil affairs. About three years later he publicly declared that the claims on which papal authority rested are ill founded in Scripture, that the pope's salvation is no more certain than any other man's, and that if the pope's life and actions do not conform to the Gospel he ought not to be obeyed.

Wyclif's doctrine of predestination provided the basis for his doctrine of the Church as the invisible body (visible and known only to God) of God's elect. Christ is the head of this society of the predestined; the pope may be the head of the Church militant on earth—but only if he is himself predestined. Any Christian's election to salvation may be judged by his obedience of the law of God, and the law of

God is in the Gospel. This explains why everybody, laymen as well as priest, should know the Bible: so that he can know who is of the elect.

Other Wyclifian tenets were these:

The pope should have no temporal power at all, since God has given all temporal power to Caesar.

There is no indelible character in holy orders; sacraments administered by a priest in mortal sin are invalid.

The doctrine of transubstantiation is false. (Wyclif's doctrine of Christ's eucharistic presence resembles the later Lutheran doctrine of consubstantiation.)

Naturally, such doctrines shocked and outraged some people, notably the papacy, the higher clergy, and the wealthier lords. In 1377 Pope Gregory XI issued several bulls condemning Wyclif's teachings, and the audacious rebel was imprisoned at Oxford. But his position was such that his enemies could not effectively prosecute him, and he died a natural death in 1384.

Wyclif's influence and cause lived on in the movement known as Lollardy. He had gathered about him a group of apostolic spirits willing to go about the land as the early friars had done, preaching the Gospel to the masses. These men were known as the Poor Preachers. They went on their mission armed with the Bible in English, which Wyclif and some associates had translated.

Lollardy was soon driven underground. It was popularly associated with political sedition, a charge which its clerical enemies eagerly pressed. But Wyclif's ideas and inspiration flowed throughout Europe, and in faraway Bohemia reached the soul of John Huss. In the end Huss died a martyr, but not before leaving a permanent mold upon the Czech national consciousness. In England, the disturbing effect of the Lollard pamphlets and preachments led to severe persecution. In 1401 the statute *De heretico comburendo* prescribed that any Lollard who refused to abjure his opinions should be tried by his bishop, and, if found guilty, be publicly burned. After about thirty years of constant persecution the movement appeared to have been effectively put down; but it kept up a vigorous underground life until the Reformation. For that revolution Lollardy played no small part in preparing the way.

[1] Robert Bridges, *The Testament of Beauty*. By permission of the Clarendon Press, Oxford.

[2] Arnold J. Toynbee, *A Study of History* (abridgement of volumes I–VI by D. C. Somervell), 352.

[3] G. G. Coulton sets out the evidence with some fullness in *Medieval Panorama*, devoting a whole chapter to the Black Death.

[4] Coulton, *Ibid*, 502.

Chapter Eight

Medieval Religion

Adam lay ibounden
  Bounden in a bond;
Four thousand winter
  Thoght he not too long;
And all was for an appil,
  An appil that he tok,
As clerkes finden
  Written in here book.
Ne hadde the appil take ben,
  The appil taken ben,
Ne hadde never our lady
  A ben hevene quene.
Blessed be the time
  That appil take was.
Therefore we moun singen
  Deo gracias.
Anonymous, early 15th century

Medieval religion, both formal theology and popular piety, was one thing throughout Western Christendom, and England was at one with France, Spain and Sweden in faith, morals, worship and devotion.

About five hundred years stand between the separation of Eastern from Western Christendom in the 11th century and the Protestant Reformation in the 16th. During this whole time there was not a single addition to the fundamental dogmas of the Church. The dogmas of the Trinity and the Incarnation had been forged in the councils of the fourth and fifth centuries. The doctrine of the eucharist was closely connected with Christology, and at the Lateran Council in 1215 was promulgated the doctrine of transubstantiation defining the mystery wherein the bread and wine by consecration become Christ's body and blood. There was a prevailing fixation of thought upon the Atonement. St. Thomas Aquinas had affirmed papal infallibility. But these were developments, not new doctrines, and seemed to be simply derivative from postulates which had been earlier established.

It is a truism that Eastern Christianity glorifies Christ in his heavenly majesty while Western Christianity glorifies him in his earthly humiliation, passion and death. This Jesucentric piety developed as the medieval era ran its course. The faithful were moved and haunted by the wounds of Jesus. Pictures of the wounded heart and bleeding body of the Savior abounded in English churches, as everywhere throughout the West. Along with this Jesus piety went a growing tenderness of feeling about the blessed virgin. In the earlier Marian iconography she had been portrayed as interceding for sinners or as showing her divine son to mankind. But in the middle ages she became more and more "Our Lady of Pity," holding in her arms the dead body of Christ.

What lay behind these devotional developments concerning both Christ and Mary was a reaction against the earlier religion of gloom and fear in which Christ had been seen as the implacable judge, not as the compassionate savior. The bleeding and dying of Jesus, the tears and heartbreak of the mother of God, were eagerly laid hold of as evidence that somehow, somewhere, in the court of heaven there is pity and fellow feeling for the poor, sinful, suffering mortal man

here below. The worship of the Crucified and the veneration
of his mother were meant to banish the terror of God. By
no means did the effort universally and consistently succeed.

The doctrine and administration of the sacraments became fixed during the 12th and 13th centuries. The Council
of Florence in 1439 gave official authority to Peter Lom-
bard's enumeration of seven: baptism, confirmation, eucharist, penance, unction, orders, and matrimony. However,
the English Franciscan Alexander of Hales (d. 1245) anticipated the later Anglican distinction between the two
greater sacraments of baptism and the eucharist and the five
lesser ones which cannot claim to have been directly insti-
tuted by Christ.

No survey of medieval religion can pass over without
notice the traffic in indulgences or "pardons." (In England
the peddlers of indulgences were known as pardoners.) The
practice grew out of the Church's earlier penitential system,
and becomes understandable enough if as one studies it he
bears in mind man's need for both mercy and justice. The
penitent was assured that he was forgiven, as had been the
great prototypal penitents Moses and David after their
sinning; but Moses and David, so related the Scriptures, had
had to suffer some temporal punishment, and so must he.
Justice demanded it. It was better to take his punishment
while still in the flesh and get it over with, rather than later,
in purgatory. The Church could mitigate the painful punishment he really deserved by drawing "credit" for him from
the inexhaustible treasury of merit built up by the super-
abundant goodness of Christ and his saints. From this
treasury the popes at first drew "partial" indulgences or re-
missions of punishment, and later "plenary" or complete
indulgences. A later development made it possible for Christians on earth to secure indulgences for souls in purgatory.
A gift of money to the Church became acceptable, then
normal, as a "petition" for an indulgence. Thus were provided the makings of an abuse which would do much to

wreck the unity of the Church. Thomas Gascoigne, the chancellor of Oxford, wrote around 1450:

Sinners say nowadays, "I care not how many or how great sins I commit before God, for I most easily and quickly get plenary remission of any guilt or penalty whatever by absolution and indulgence granted to me from the pope, whose writing and grant I have bought for 4d. or 6d. or for a game of tennis."

Christian nurture

In any age it is the Church's business to provide means of grace and growth for the Christian soul. If we could visit a typical English parish of the 14th or 15th century we should find the following order of things.

Infants were usually baptized on the day of their birth. Along with the baptismal rite there was an elaborate ritual of exorcism, anointing, and clothing the infant in the white chrisom cloth. The child was confirmed while still in infancy, if at all; this sacrament was widely neglected.

Marriage began at the church door and the rite culminated in the nuptial mass. The priest visited the couple in their marriage bed and sprinkled them with holy water. Despite the solemnity with which the Church invested the marriage rite, the holy estate of matrimony was commonly degraded by the sacrifice of all other considerations to financially advantageous unions. Many people, on coming of age, entered marriages which had been arranged years before by their parents.

Sacramental confession was part of one's preparation for holy communion. There is good reason to believe that its healthy and helpful use was the rule among the common folk in England.

By the late middle ages holy unction, which had earlier been primarily the sacrament of healing, had degenerated

into "extreme" unction—little more than a preparation for
death.

The center and focus of worship was the mass; but for
the layman the mass was something to be seen and heard
rather than actively shared in and received. The ordinary
layman received holy communion only a few times in the
year, often only at Easter.

The Bible was virtually unknown to the layman, for two
reasons. First, he could seldom read. Secondly, the Bible
was a very expensive book before the invention of the print-
ing press in the middle of the 15th century, and even then
remained beyond the financial reach of most people. The
ordinary worshiper gained some knowledge of the biblical
saga of salvation indirectly, from sermons, from religious
drama, and from pictures in his church.

To dwell upon the superstitions which bedevilled the
medieval Christian is depressing and otiose, but they cannot
be omitted from an honest accounting. It is often said that
a little superstition can't hurt anybody much, but that a
little unbelief can. The fallacy in this idea is the assumption
that "a little superstition" is merely a harmless and perhaps
charming companion of true faith. But a real superstition is
a pernicious substitute for true faith; a foe, not a friend. One
example from medieval annals may illustrate: the case of the
woman who kept a consecrated host in her mouth at mass,
carried it home, and placed it in a bee-hive to reduce mor-
tality among the bees. According to the story it worked; and
not only that: the bees "built for their most sweet Guest,
out of their sweetest honeycombs, a tiny chapel of mar-
velous workmanship."[1] Here superstition has blocked the
channel of grace. What the poor woman receives from the
blessed sacrament (assuming the pretty story to be true) is
a miracle that must be the talk of the county. But the true
miracle of the mass is the divine gift of conformity to Christ
and union with him. It is impossible to believe that, in this
instance, the woman put the important thing first. Super-

stition and saving faith can never be friends; the one is a
malignant parasite upon the other.

During the medieval period, superstition was rife on all
levels of society, but this is by no means the whole spiritual
story of the age. The age was in truth full of paradoxes and
contradictions. The French historian Daniel-Rops writes:

> This age of large-scale massacres is also one of great mystical
> impulses; the odor of blood and roses hangs over it, inextricably
> mingled. It is the age of macabre dances and of exquisitely deli-
> cate miniatures, of witchcraft trials and the *Imitation of Christ*.
> The thirst for pleasure goes hand in hand with the taste for
> excessive penance, and those very men whom we see possessed
> by such savage violence are also perfectly capable of astonishing
> flights towards sanctity. It is a morbid, feverish epoch, in which
> the noblest spiritual impulses turn all too easily to neurosis. Even
> the Christian is caught in the toils of the powerful emotions
> which he is straining after, and seems to waver. Everything every-
> where is changing and falling apart; systems oppose systems, the
> new dogmatisms clash with the old; rigid formulae only half
> conceal all the uncertainty and anguish. The whole of human
> activity is held increasingly fast in the grip of an indefinable kind
> of agonizing fermentation.[2]

Mystics

This age of large-scale massacres was indeed an age of
deep mystical impulses, and Christian mysticism reached
notable heights in some English men and women. Among
these was Richard Rolle (*c.* 1300–49), who strongly influenced Wyclif. In protest against the formalism and worldliness of contemporary monasticism he chose to live as a
hermit. In describing his experiences of union with God,
Rolle uses the imageries of heat, sweetness, and song. He is
one of the first religious writers to write in English as well as
Latin. In an age of regimentation, he was a doughty champion of liberty of conscience and personal inspiration.

Walter Hilton (d. 1396) was deeply influenced by Rolle. He earnestly concerned himself with the spiritual life of common folk living in the world. His *Epistle on Mixed Life* is a guide for such people, and foreshadows such later English devotional writings as William Law's *Serious Call to a Devout and Holy Life* (1728).

The first English literary woman known to us is Julian of Norwich (*c.* 1343–*c.* 1413). An anchoress who lived in a cell in a churchyard, she had little learning but deep and holy wisdom. In a pessimistic age, her word from the Lord to His people was that although "sin is behovable (necessary), we are nevertheless to be sure that all shall be well, and all manner of thing shall be well."

Theologians

Enough has already been said about John Wyclif to indicate that he was one Englishman of the 14th century of first-rate intellect who dared to think, and to think aloud, very independently of ecclesiastical authority. He was not alone in this, although historically he enjoys and merits a special eminence. The impact of the Black Death, combined with other developments such as the failure of the Cluniac reform to achieve its goals and the triumph of worldliness in many ways and places, served to turn the movement of philosophy into new directions. A strong rival of Wyclif in his theological influence upon his own contemporaries and upon later thinkers was William Occam (*c.* 1300–*c.* 1349), the *Doctor Invincibilis*. He was a Franciscan who studied and taught at Oxford, where he was accused by the chancellor of the university of teaching dangerous doctrines. In championing the cause of the "Spirituals" in his order, who taught and practiced an absolute rule of poverty, he came into conflict with Pope John XXII, by whom he was excommunicated in 1328. Undaunted by this, he continued to

write treatises on various dangerous subjects, among these
being the question of the nature of the Christian society and
the proper powers of the *imperium* and the *sacerdotium*—
the old, continuing question on which William I and Gregory VII had divided. Occam, along with his Italian contemporary Marsiglio of Padua, followed a line which could
only be called pro-imperial and anti-papal. He argued that
the Church should be radically separated from the world,
denied the pope all temporal authority, and exalted the role
of the laity. His political theories helped to prepare the way
for the modern concept of the state.

Occam was profoundly influential in both philosophy and
theology. In philosophy, for example, he was an advocate
of rigorous nominalism and thus a forerunner of modern
British empiricism. In theology, he assailed the scholastic
fusion of faith with reason, as classically formulated by
Aquinas, and his exaltation of faith as man's sole means of
knowing God was to be taken up and carried farther by
Martin Luther.

Because the ideas of Occam and his followers seemed to
smack of Pelagianism they were answered by an Oxford contemporary, Thomas Bradwardine, who became Archbishop
of Canterbury. His conviction of the need for divine grace
for salvation was so powerful that it led him into a theological determinism which may have helped to shape John
Wyclif's full predestinarianism. Theologically, Bradwardine
anticipates and foreshadows Calvin, although there is no
evidence that Calvin drew upon his theology as a source.

The suppression of heresy

The "establishment" in both church and state in the
second half of the 14th century was disturbed by the bold
new doctrines of Wyclif and others, and by the fact that
some of these doctrines at any rate were clearly subversive

of the established order. The Church leaders counter-attacked. Their first step was the condemnation of Wyclif's teachings on the eucharist, at Oxford, in 1381. The next year William Courtenay, Archbishop of Canterbury, convened a council in London at which 24 propositions from Wyclif's writings were condemned. Under Courtenay's rule at Canterbury and that of his successor, Thomas Arundel, a stern inquisitorial policy of extirpating heresy at Oxford and other "infested" areas was carried on, usually with royal support. The program seemed to accomplish its purpose, until in 1413 Sir John Oldcastle, a convicted Lollard, escaped from prison, rounded up a small army of followers, and frightened authorities with the threat of an armed assault upon London.

Faced by the radical prophets, reformers, and revisionists of theology, like Wyclif, the powers of church and state seem to have drawn together as allies against a common foe, and this may be the primary reason why the breakdown of the medieval synthesis of *imperium* and *sacerdotium* did not take place earlier than it did. Christendom was not ready for the revolution which would take place in the 16th century. But as the middle age grew senescent it grew less serene, more troubled. To quote Daniel-Rops again:

Anguish, exaltation and derangement: the historian who attempts to pinpoint the dominant characteristics of faith at the close of the Middle Ages finds himself forced to return to these words again and again. He is confronted with a state of religious agitation which manifests itself in various forms, and with an intense ferment of mysticism, both orthodox and heterodox in character. It is exceedingly hard to recognize here any of the stable, tranquil faith of the twelfth and thirteenth centuries, where the most striking flights towards holiness had something serene and reserved about them, and where even superstition retained some gleam of common sense and sanctity. By and large William James's phrase, 'a theopathic state,' is an apt description of this decadent society, a society in which the elements of a bygone greatness were in an advanced state of decomposition.[3]

[1] Recorded by Caesar of Heisterbach and quoted by Will Durant, *The Age of Faith*, 737.
[2] H. Daniel-Rops, *The Protestant Reformation*, 107.
[3] *Ibid*, 115.

Chapter Nine

The Flaring of Mankind

Why, to be Luther—that's a life to lead,
Incomparably better than my own.
He comes, reclaims God's earth for God, he says,
Sets up God's rule again by simple means,
Reopens a shut book, and all is done.
He flared out in the flaring of mankind;
Such Luther's luck was. . . .
Robert Browning, *Bishop Blougram's Apology*

The worldly-wise bishop is right in saying that Luther "flared out in the flaring of mankind." The world into which Luther came was ready to flare. What had made it so, the preconditions of the Protestant Reformation, combined to make some such revolution inevitable, and Luther, Calvin, and the other eminent leaders, who made history, were also made by history.

We have noted some of the facts and factors that prepared the way. The great frustration resulting from the failure of the Cluniac movement to bring about the regeneration of the world which its ardent adherents longed for; the erosion of general trust in the beneficence and soundness of the established ordering of religion and society which followed the Black Death; the teachings of prophets and rebels like Wyclif which found their way to many minds

before they could be suppressed. These we have already
noted. Along with them other major preconditions of the
Reformation should be kept in mind to provide perspective
on the "flaring."

Nationalism in its modern sense was emerging, slowly but
certainly. This development profoundly affected the papal
monarchy in Europe, for as the nations took shape their
rulers and governments grew in effective power. A most
crucial showdown took place early in the 14th century when
King Philip IV of France claimed the right to tax the
Church within his land to support his war against England.
Pope Boniface VIII condemned this procedure. Philip retaliated by seizing the pope and holding him prisoner. The
point that registered with all the world was that the king got
away with it. The next step was the capture not simply of an
individual pope but of the papacy as such, by the French
crown, when the papacy was moved to Avignon.

Some seventy years later the papacy returned to Rome,
but some cardinals had come to prefer residence in Avignon.
What resulted from this was the scandal of schism within
the papacy itself, with rival popes of Rome and Avignon
openly at war with each other. This demoralizing situation
lasted for nearly forty years. It meant the final breakdown
of papal monarchy as a single central authority which could
hold the whole realm of Christendom together in Christian
peace and unity.

The papal schism made the most thoughtful men realize
that radical reform was necessary, and out of this came what
is known as the conciliar movement. The conciliarists decided that the one thing that could save the Church was a
general council, along the lines of such great Christian assemblies in earlier times as Nicea and Chalcedon. But such
a council could not lawfully be held in the middle ages unless a pope convened it, and the conciliarists realized that
any council thus convened and controlled by a pope could
hardly be free to reform the papacy. However, some bold
souls, including cardinals of both papal camps, resolved to

go ahead with a council. There would be three such assemblies in the 15th century.

The first met at Pisa in 1409. Neither pope recognized its
authority. The council declared both popes deposed, thus
asserting the authority of a council over the papacy. It then
elected a new pope. But the result was a fiasco, for now there
were three claimants to the papal throne where there had
been two. The second council was held in Florence in 1414–
1418. This was more successful. It was able at last to end
the papal pluralism, and under Pope Martin V (1417–1431)
Roman Christendom had once more a single ruler. The
council declared in effect that the papacy is a constitutional
monarchy, not absolute, and that the pope as executive head
of the Church is to be regulated by the legislation of proper
Church councils. However, as soon as the council disbanded
the pope was free to repudiate its decrees. The third council,
held intermittently at Basel from 1431 to 1449, tried to
effect numerous constitutional and administrative reforms
along lines begun at Florence. But the popes were able to
nullify the proposals that came out of such councils by
various expedients, one of these being the making of various
concordats with civil powers. In the world of that time, if
a pope and a king agreed on something within that king's
realm there was nothing that the Church, apart from the
pope, could do to prevent it. So the conciliar movement
failed, ultimately, because there was no effective power to
back up the councils.

The Renaissance

The rich and complex movement known as the Renaissance was born in Italy. It captured the papacy itself to the
extent that all the popes from 1447 to 1521 were humanists
strongly favoring this "new birth" of the ancient classical

culture. Coming at the time that it did, this movement appeared as an emancipation from the moral restraints of Christianity, and by it many Christians were "emancipated" into a life of licentious immorality. This corrupting phase of the Renaissance hurt the Church by making paganism attractive to many Church leaders. Thus a religious reaction against the corrupted Church was made inevitable. The Reformation was, in part, that reaction. Owen Chadwick rightly remarks: "The Reformation came not so much because Europe was irreligious as because it was religious."[1] Too often, both defenders and critics of the late medieval Church overlook the obvious; that is, that if there was dreadful corruption in that Church there were also in that Church very religious people who attacked the corruption. Savonarola, Wyclif, Luther, and other such scourges of the Lord were not Hindus.

Too commonly also it is suggested that the Renaissance was sheer calamity to Christianity. It would be easy to cite a hundred contrary facts, but one should be enough. The Dutch humanist Erasmus (c. 1466–1536) was a Renaissance man. He wanted to put the Bible into the hands of every man, reason to replace superstition, and simplicity and moral integrity to be the rule of all religion. His was the Renaissance mind and spirit in Christian action, and no reasonable critic today would question that it was a spirit which the Church always needs.

In approaching the Reformation it is well to take note that it was a many-sided revolution, in which no less than six major and distinct movements can be traced. They may be identified as follows:

(1) The reformation within the Roman Church itself, commonly known as the Counter-Reformation. This was conservative in that it involved no theological innovation but rather a codification of western catholic doctrine as it stood at the end of the middle ages. Along with this went a thorough administrative re-organization, a strengthening of

discipline, an enhancement of papal power, and a tremendous missionary effort.

(2) The Lutheran movement; also comparatively conservative, primarily a rediscovery of the Bible and a proclamation of Luther's doctrine of justification by faith.

(3) The Calvinist-Zwinglian movement, more radical than Luther's; its key doctrine was the sovereignty of God with all that this implies—according to John Calvin.

(4) The anabaptist movement farther over to the radical left, aiming not at reforming the old Church but at creating a new Church composed only of the elect believers in Christ.

(5) The humanist movement, of which Erasmus was the father. He never left the Roman Church but acted as a satirical critic from within, apparently hoping to ridicule it into reform. This movement was the ancestor of such ultra-liberal Christianities as the Socinian and Unitarian. Its key doctrine sees Jesus not as man's divine Savior but as man's perfect human example.

(6) The English reformation, related in various ways to all the foregoing movements but identical with none of them. Its several peculiar characteristics will be noted later.

Immediate background

The Church of the Renaissance era is commonly pictured as very wealthy. But if wealth is what one has in the bank the Church was in fact closer to bankruptcy, which explains, to give one example, why in 1484 Pope Innocent VIII had to pawn his tiara for 100,000 ducats. The cost of administering the Church was constantly rising and so the popes had to raise the price for such services as dispensations, exemptions and bulls of indulgence. The hard financial facts helped to set the stage for Luther's challenge.

Archbishop Albert was a German prince who was also Archbishop of Mainz, Archbishop of Magdeburg, and administrator of the see of Halberstadt. He could hold all these offices at once only by papal dispensation. He could pay for the dispensation only by borrowing from the German banking house known as the Fugger of Augsburg. As security for the loan, he promised to promote throughout Germany an indulgence which the pope had recently declared. The pope needed money to build St. Peter's Cathedral; Albert needed money to repay his bankers. A successful sale of the indulgence would yield money for the needs of both. One of the best men in the indulgence business (and it was that) was put in charge: the Dominican Johann Tetzel. The Elector Frederick, ruler of Saxony, forbade the sale of the indulgence within his realm, but he could not prevent his people from going to hear Tetzel preach in neighboring towns. It was Tetzel's crusade that roused Martin Luther to attack. Luther at this time (1517) was a professor of Holy Scripture at the University of Wittenburg. He had been thinking, and agonizing, about the nature of salvation, and had concluded that salvation is purely a gift of God's grace which man can never earn, deserve, or buy, but can only humbly receive. It was claimed that by purchasing the indulgence one could help one's soul, or the soul of another, to attain salvation. This struck Luther as blasphemous. He preached openly against it and on October 31, 1517, posted his famous 95 theses on the door of the castle church which was the university bulletin board. His statement was restrained and cautious in tone, meant to stimulate academic discussion rather than to ignite a revolution. Luther did not deny the right of the pope to grant indulgences. Rather, he challenged the extension of the power of indulgences to purgatory. But Tetzel took up the challenge and the theological war was on. In the course of it Luther would eventually deny the sovereign jurisdiction of the pope over the Church and would make Holy Scripture the sole rule of faith. The Church of England would follow him in this, but would never become Lutheran in doctrine and practice. To

speculate about what might have happened in England if
Luther had not "happened" in Germany is interesting but
quite idle.

Other reformers

Huldreich Zwingli, a Swiss contemporary of Luther, was
eminently a Christian humanist, a friend and kindred spirit
of Erasmus. He was also, however, a radical biblicist who
believed that only the Bible is binding upon the Christian
conscience. He argued, for example, that because the Lenten
fast is not enjoined by Holy Scripture no Christian is obli-
gated to observe it. The more conservative Luther held that
church customs which do not contradict Scripture should
be retained. Anglicanism would follow Luther in this principle, while English puritanism would follow Zwingli.
Protestantism as the religion of "the Bible only" begins with
Zwingli.

The continental movement which would be most influential in England was Calvinism, stemming from the
mind and work of the Frenchman John Calvin (1509-64).
Lutheranism never seriously threatened to capture the
Church of England; Calvinism did.

Calvin started with Luther's essential doctrine of justification by faith, which would be more accurately described by
the more cumbersome title of justification by grace through
faith. What both Luther and Calvin were proclaiming is
that sinful man is made acceptable to God, not by anything
he himself is or does but solely by God's loving grace. This
grace is freely offered to all men, but only as man has faith
(personal trust) in God can he receive this grace and be
justified—reconciled and restored to God—by it.

Calvin began with this premise. To it he added his own
concept of the absolute sovereignty of God, which was a
revival of the Hebrew idea expressed by Job in his question:
"Shall we receive good at the hand of God, and shall we not

receive evil?" (Job 2:10) *All* things are of God, the damnation of the reprobate no less than the salvation of the elect. To deny this is to deny God's omnipotence, omniscience and rule. If God chooses to damn a man that man is damned, and the man himself can do nothing about it. If a man goes to heaven or to hell it is solely because God so willed it. This seems a grim doctrine, considered by itself; but to Calvin and his followers it was in actual effect a source of comfort and confidence. It enabled a man to say that if God had elected him to salvation he could not possibly end up among the lost, since what God wills cannot fail.

If man's salvation is entirely a matter of God's decreeing and not at all a matter of man's striving or doing, there would logically seem to be no need or place for the Church. Why have a hospital for sinners, or dispensary of saving grace, if man is simply saved or simply damned by God's inscrutable and irreversible decree? But Calvin thought his way through to a strong churchmanship, albeit a distinct and different one from the traditional catholic concept of the Church. The Romanist saw the Church as a visible institution with a hierarchical order, ruled by the pope as Christ's vicar on earth. On this view the Church is a mixed body of saints and sinners. Luther saw the Church as the body of true believers: one belongs to it not by having been baptized but by having faith. Because faith is invisible the Church is visible only to him who can "see" the faith of its members, which only God can fully see. For Calvin, membership is even more invisible, for the Church is the "universal number of the elect" and only God knows who are the elect. This principle puts the Church, as J. S. Whale remarks, "beyond the sight and reach of all ecclesiastical officials and institutions: God's elect may even be outside the Church as formally organized, and many inside it may not be, in fact, of the elect. As St. Augustine had put it: 'There are many sheep without and many wolves within.' "[2]

Although, on Calvin's view, only God can know who are His elect, yet these elect will be discernible by their purity of life and good works. This provides a basis for a visible church, a community of believers; but such a body will resemble more an army of saints, sure of their election and showing forth the fruits of faith in godly living, than it will resemble the catholic mixed body of good and bad. Moreover, in Calvin's church the basis of authority is not clerical status; if the lowliest member is right with God and the most exalted member is wrong with God the former should bear rule over the latter. Here was the seed of the later protestant idea that the man called to the ministry must be called to his pastorate by the congregation he will serve. No hierarchical polity, not even a simplified episcopacy, can rest upon this principle. The Church of England would find that it could not embrace Calvinism and retain episcopacy.

Calvin's "rule of the saints" in Geneva had a wide, deep, and lasting influence which is felt to this day. The protestantism of France, Holland, Scotland, and English puritanism stems directly from it. Calvinism showed a tremendous ability to unite its adherents against the most hostile civil powers. It produced men who, strong in the assurance of their divine election, could face without flinching all the wiles of the devil and cruelties of men.

England as a whole did not become Calvinist ecclesiastically, but the Calvinist spirit entered the nation's spiritual blood-stream. Calvinism helped prepare the way for the modern democratic state in England and elsewhere, largely by producing a temper in men which made them defy earthly potentates whom they judged ungodly or who, in their judgment, were infringing upon God's sovereign prerogatives.

[1] Owen Chadwick, *The Reformation.*
[2] J. S. Whale, *The Protestant Tradition*, 147.

Chapter Ten

The King's Matter

The historian must beware of confusing a man's cause or party or religion with his character.

David Knowles

The English historian Powicke called the English reformation an act of state, which it essentially was. Its occasion,
though not its cause, was what was known as "the king's
matter" at the time when it was current: the demand of
King Henry VIII for an annulment of his marriage with
Catharine of Aragon. Too many people evidently imagine
that the English reformation was all of Henry's doing, but
the truth is that very little of it took place during his lifetime.
Too many swallow the pure-nonsense theory that this lusty
and ruthless monarch "created" the Church of England so
that he could get rid of one wife and take another—and then
another, and then another.

The most that can be truthfully said of Henry's part in
the reformation is that it got started under him and because
of him.

The causes of unrest which had been working throughout
Europe in the late middle ages were operative in England
as well. The English bishops had become primarily feudal
landlords rather than shepherds of the flock. The monastic
houses had suffered a gradual deterioration to the extent that
as the 16th century opened there was some flagrant moral

corrupton in them but much more sheer complacent worldliness. Some of the houses possessed enormous wealth in
land and revenues, and it could hardly be said by their most
devoted advocates that they justified their affluence by their
good works and care for the poor. And there was more bitter
resentment of the papal taxation than ever before. England
had come to be known as "the milk cow of the papacy" as
a source of revenue. As the spirit of nationalism waxed, so
did the sense of grievance against the papacy as a "foreign
power."

There were subterranean currents of doctrinal dissent
which grew stronger and bolder after Luther had launched
his movement in Germany. Lollardy had never been totally
suppressed in England, and the fact that in 1512 Archbishop
Warham of Canterbury found it necessary to summon a
convocation to deal with heresy would indicate that heresy
was growing apace. Then Lutheran ideas invaded the land,
secretly of course, but effectively. Among the learned and influential there were men like John Colet, Dean of St. Paul's,
who boldly championed reform. Colet is the most eminent
but he was not alone. He had no thought of a break with
the established papal order, but vigorously attacked the
worldliness of the higher clergy. A close friend of Erasmus,
Colet was one of the Renaissance luminaries at Oxford,
where as early as 1497 he lectured on the Epistles of St. Paul
in a critical spirit, and in the light of the Pauline doctrines
called for a return to the spirit and purity of the primitive
Church. Colet openly taught that the office of the papacy
was not essential to the Church.

Erasmus taught at Oxford, and his influence toward a
new kind of theological scholarship, based upon a critical
study of the foundations of the faith in the Holy Scriptures,
was felt not only in the university but throughout the land
—not as a mass appeal, but in the minds of the more
thoughtful. At Cambridge the new ideas associated with the
new learning seem to have taken even deeper hold than at
Oxford.

It is important to grasp the fact that reform was in the air of England before the king's matter became the *casus belli*.

Henry came to the throne in 1509, at 17. As a boy he had been intended for the Church and had been an avid young theologian. The death of his brother Arthur in 1502 made him heir apparent to the throne. From the outset of his reign Henry was admired and loved by his people. Here was a king who "had everything": youth, charm, intelligence, a wide range of ardent enthusiasms for sports, poetry, music and the arts. Fatefully, he had also an imperious natural determination to have his own way in all things. He is one of history's purest autocrats.

In the early years of Henry's reign, the most powerful executive in England was not the king but his chancellor, Cardinal Wolsey, who was also the pope's plenipotentiary legate. From 1518 to 1528 Wolsey in effect ruled England. He was a genius in statecraft but not in public relations. Through his grandiose living, craftiness, rapacity and his very successes, he made himself increasingly unpopular. In the eyes of the lay public Wolsey represented the papal power and the pomp and arrogance of the higher clergy. When it became convenient, Henry would be able to turn the general anti-Wolseyism into anti-papalism and anti-clericalism. Had Wolsey been a more appealing figure to the masses, the English reformation could not have taken the direction that it did, and certainly Henry would not have fared so successfully in his anti-papal enterprises. When Wolsey fell, the prestige of the papacy fell.

Henry had married his brother Arthur's widow Catharine, a princess of Aragon. Pope Julius II had been persuaded to grant a dispensation for the union. This was needed because at that time a man was not ordinarily allowed to marry his deceased brother's wife. Henry and Catharine had been married for 18 years when he became deeply anxious about the fact that of the five children she had borne him none of the males had survived infancy. She was now forty, surely near

or at the end of her child-bearing. The king began to wonder
if God was punishing him for his unlawful marriage. To be
sure, Christ's vicar on earth had allowed it. But there was
that troubling verse in Holy Scripture that the theologians
kept talking about: "If a man shall take his brother's wife, it
is an unclean thing: he hath uncovered his brother's nakedness; they shall be childless." (Leviticus 20:21) Moreover,
it was not a purely personal matter. The lack of a male heir
to the throne posed a threat to the Tudor dynasty and so to
the peace and order of the realm. England could ill afford
an internecine war for the throne. There was the princess
Mary, a promising child, but a female. England had not yet
known a queen like Elizabeth I or Victoria, to rule "victo-
rious, happy and glorious," and the idea of a ruling queen
was then unthinkable. Most troubling was the thought that
Mary might take as her husband a foreign prince who would
rule the land. Henry and his countrymen had become altogether too nationalistic to tolerate such a prospect.

This political and dynastic crisis was the primary mover
of the king's matter. He had moral misgivings about his
union with Catharine, which was a supporting factor. And
he had fallen in love with Anne Boleyn, a lady of the court,
which was also a consideration, but a very secondary one.
It was quite the usual thing for a monarch of that age to
engage in such dalliance, and if it was just Anne's body he
wanted he could have kept her as his mistress. The decisive
fact was his determination to be free to marry a woman who
could bear children, so that he could sire a male heir within
wedlock who would be legitimate.

What was needed to clear the way was a papal indult to
nullify the union with Catharine, and he set Wolsey to the
task of getting it done. Wolsey had little stomach for it but
he tried. He failed, and it was a fatal failure for him. The
then pope, Clement VII, was in a most difficult position.
Politically he was in the power of the emperor, Charles V.
The emperor was Catharine's nephew, and made it clear
that if the pope ruled against his aunt he would be danger-

ously displeased. Clement played for time, hoping for a break; but the only break that finally came was between Rome and England.

After waiting two years, Henry lost patience with Wolsey, decided that Wolsey had outlived his usefulness and must be ditched. It was done with deadly ease. Wolsey was charged with violating the Statute of Praemunire (1392) which forbade any Englishman to take orders from a foreign power. Wolsey was accused of doing this as the pope's legate. It was true that the king himself had urged him to obtain this legatine authority, and Wolsey had used it largely to serve the king's ends; but this fact was simply ignored. In 1530 Wolsey was arrested for high treason and died before he could be brought to trial.

By 1531 Henry had vainly waited four years for a papal decision. He was rid of Wolsey but he could not be sure of how all the clergy of the realm would stand in a showdown between king and pope. To shackle them, he charged all English clergy with violation of Praemunire, because they had accepted Wolsey as papal legate. To escape punishment they had to meet two conditions: payment of a fine of 100,000 pounds, and acknowledgement of Henry as "Protector and Supreme Head of the English Church and Clergy." They paid the fine—thus in effect confessing their "crime," but they could not stomach the title. Henry gave some ground and chose to settle for the less sublime title of "Singular Protector, only and supreme Lord, and, as far as the law of Christ allows, even Supreme Head" of the English Church.

All this was not sheer megalomania. Henry knew that in past ages there had been Christian rulers like Justinian, Charlemagne, and William the Conqueror who saw themselves as the divinely anointed lawgivers within their realms. He asserted his place in their company. For centuries the pope had claimed to be the universal judge of Christendom, and cases had been appealed from the king's courts to the pope's as from lower to higher. Henry now challenged this practice, declaring that the pope's jurisdiction in England was usurped and demanding that it be abolished. In claiming to be Supreme Head, under Christ, of the English Church, he claimed no spiritual headship. "Supreme Head" is a legal term. The pope's supremacy in matters of doctrine and church order was not being questioned; what was being repudiated was the pope's claim to the right to proclaim and to enforce law in England through his own courts rather than through the king's courts. Moreover, Henry clearly considered that as Supreme Head he was the proper judge of what *was* sound doctrine and practice in the Church.

Henry received eager help from Parliament toward his goal of royal supremacy. Many of its members were anticlerical. By a series of enactments the power of the bishops and clergy was effectively undercut, the flow of money to Rome was reduced to a trickle, and legal appeals to Rome were outlawed. But Henry was forced to stain his hands with the blood of two illustrious men who were martyrs for the old regime. Bishop John Fisher of Rochester, alone of the whole bench of bishops, refused to take the oath of the royal supremacy. Such refusal was adjudged to be treason. While Fisher was in prison for his refusal the pope appointed him as cardinal. This probably sealed his doom; he was convicted and executed in 1535. The other saintly martyr at the king's hands was Sir Thomas More. Henry had admired and loved him, and had appointed him as chancellor succeeding Wolsey. But More could not accommodate the king's desire for a chancellor who would press for the annulment of the marriage. He was against it, and simply refused to act. Moreover, he could not take the oath of supremacy. The king had no other choice than to prosecute him for treason, and More went to the block a few weeks after Fisher.

The blood of these martyrs could not stem the tide.

Wolsey had failed and More had refused to secure the annulment. In the summer of 1530, Henry met Thomas Cranmer, a shy and unambitious Cambridge don, who sug-

gested that the question of the lawfulness of the union of
Henry and Catharine be submitted to the universities of
England and the continent in a kind of opinion poll of the
academic theologians. The results would presumably carry
some weight with the pope. Actually, the results were in-
decisive. The answers from Italy were split; the Lutheran
universities on the continent voted against Henry; the University of Paris voted for him. Oxford and Cambridge went
down the line for their king, but only after being threatened.

Henry made Cranmer Archbishop of Canterbury in 1533.
The appointment was entirely satisfactory to the pope, who
bestowed the pallium upon Cranmer. In fact, Cranmer retained full papal recognition and acceptance as archbishop
until he was deposed under Mary. Cranmer sincerely believed in the royal supremacy. He differed from the king on
only one important issue, but he kept his dissent to himself
for so long as Henry lived. They disagreed about the reforming theologies, both Lutheran and Calvinist. Henry would
have none of it. In his beliefs he was a medieval catholic,
despite his willingness to use protestant forces to his own
ends, and remained so to the end. Cranmer was drawn to
the protestant movement and began to think along protestant lines as soon as he encountered the thought of the
reformers.

In 1534 several acts of Parliament conveyed formerly
papal powers to either the king or the archbishop. The Succession Act was passed, legally sanctioning Henry's divorce
from Catharine and authorizing him to demand an oath of
allegiance of any subject. Thus the papal jurisdiction in
England, which had lasted for almost a thousand years, was
swept away in a moment. And the Church of England itself
played no active part in this at all. The initiative, the impetus, the resolve, were all Henry's, and Parliament was his
willing partner.

How the masses of people felt about it we have no way of
knowing. Of course they were not consulted. The nobles and
the more affluent business men were in agreement with the

king. All the bishops, except Fisher, took the oath of allegiance, which is an impressive fact. It may have been because the king was not in any way changing the Church's doctrine and worship.

By 1535 Henry badly needed money, and the easiest source lay ready at hand in the monasteries and the monastic estates. The story of the plundering and dissolution of the monasteries is shameful to recall. Monasticism had degenerated, and it can be argued that the new day called for a re-direction of the devotion and the wealth that had been poured into the religious orders. But there is no evidence that Henry had any motive other than lining his own pockets. Along with the plundering of the monasteries went a general assault upon shrines, carried on by people infected with the new protestant ideas. The most spectacular act of iconoclasm was at the king's own behest: the destruction of the shrine of Thomas Becket at Canterbury. Henry well remembered the story of the martyr-saint who had defied a king, and judged that it was time for him to be decanonized. The shrine was destroyed, the saint's bones were scattered, and his name stricken from all church kalendars.

It seems that Henry was entirely willing to let the new protestant ideas and enterprises flourish in England so long as they served his purposes. He did not embrace them himself. But if, for example, the protestant zeal against sacred shrines could be used to rid him of the troublesome cult of St. Thomas Becket, with all its inconvenient political implications, he was most willing to let it roll on; indeed, he even gave it a push in the desired direction.

A much more important incident of this sort resulted in the first lawful and public English Bible. William Tyndale was dedicated to producing an English version of the Bible, but had to work at it secretly because the church authorities forbade it. In 1524 he fled to Germany where he finished his work, smuggling pages of it into England in bales of wool. He was never able to return to England but suffered martyrdom in Holland. His dying prayer was "Lord, open the King of England's eyes." The king's eyes had been opened some time before, in the sense intended by Tyndale. Since 1529 he had been interested in the production of an English Bible. A man who had worked some with Tyndale, Miles Coverdale, was set to work on the project with royal protection. In 1538 the Great Bible, based on the work of Tyndale and Coverdale, was produced, and from this time onward it was possible, as it had not been before, to study the Scriptures in English without fear of punishment. Henry, being a friend of the new learning, undoubtedly wanted to open the Bible to general reading in the vernacular. But here was another issue in which a dynamic protestant principle was at work, undermining the old ecclesiastical order; and it was pleasing in Henry's sight.

To return to the king's matter: Henry had secretly married Anne Boleyn in January 1533. Cranmer was consecrated archbishop the following March, and in May he presided at an ecclesiastical court and ruled Henry's marriage to Catharine null and void. In September Anne bore the princess Elizabeth. Henry soon tired of Anne, and in May 1536 she was charged with adultery and promptly beheaded. Whether she was guilty is anybody's guess. The king was ready for his next marital venture; eleven days after Anne's execution he married Jane Seymour. She bore him a son, the future boy-king Edward, then died a few days later. To trace Henry's later amours would be pointless. The man who had begun his reign with such shining promise had sunk into surly, ruthless mania.

What he did, and did not do, concerning the Church is of primary relevance to our purpose. Although as "Supreme Head" he never tried to exercise spiritual sovereignty, yet he saw himself as the arbiter of what was to be believed and done in the Church. He was resolved to keep all the reforming opinions out. To that end the Six Articles Act was issued in 1539; this was a royal decree of things necessary to be believed. These included specifically transubstantiation, communion in one kind only, clerical celibacy, private masses, and the necessity of auricular confession.

Henry's death in January 1547 ended the first phase of the English reformation. In it there had been no change in basic doctrine or worship, except for the abrogation of papal dominion. The king had replaced the pope as "Supreme Head in earth of the Church of England": in principle only as the legal head, controlling the Church's temporalities, but in practice able to decide and to decree what was the true faith of the Church.

Such were the consequences to religion of the king's matter.

Chapter Eleven

Revolution

Woe to thee, O land, when thy king is a child!
Ecclesiastes 10:16

Bishop Hugh Latimer aptly made this the text of a sermon in 1549 deploring the sad estate of the land under the boy king Edward VI.

Edward began his reign at the age of nine, and died at 15. Under him England was ruled successively by two regents: the Duke of Somerset (1547–49) and the Duke of Northumberland (1549–53).

Somerset was the king's uncle, Edward Seymour, and an excellent man—intelligent, brave, compassionate toward the poor of the land. He was also a strong protestant. He was able in the name of the crown to promote protestantism and he diligently did so. He and Cranmer, working together, were able to impose whatever changes in religion they wished. One policy they adopted, that of acting through Parliament rather than through the Church Convocation and the bishops, powerfully strengthened the new order which Henry had begun in which royal supremacy replaced papal supremacy.

The word went abroad that England was now a safe haven for protestants. Many English protestant refugees returned from Europe, and along with them came continental reformers hoping to find in England a protestant brave new world. Among these was a wide diversity of views. No one man, at this stage or any other, dominated the English reformation theologically.

London was the seething center of English protestantism, and there especially the frenzy of the more radical protestants against crucifixes, shrines, paintings, statues, and all such physical relics of the old order wrought wide destruction. This was iconoclasm for conscience' sake. Side by side with it went a systematic looting and plundering of the churches by people whose motive was self-enrichment. Somebody gets rich out of any revolution, and this was a revolution. But to say that this greed was the prime mover of the English reformation, as some have said, is as groundless as it is cynical. Among these first English reformers were leaders who would grace any age or movement.

One such was Hugh Latimer (1492–1555). He was no strong, stable theologian. His mind, like Cranmer's, was in constant flux on doctrinal issues. He was primarily a moral reformer. In his sermons we hear the voice of a prophet with a passion for social righteousness. England was undergoing an economic revolution along with the religious. What had for ages been common land was being seized by rich landlords who were turning this arable land into pasture land for sheep. This meant that far fewer peasants could live off the land. Latimer denounced as a violation of true religion the toleration of the cruel consequences of such economic changes.

Another impressive figure was Nicholas Ridley, who became Bishop of London in 1550. In superficial historical accounts of his age Ridley is commonly remembered, more or less patronizingly, as a fanatic who crusaded against stone altars in order to replace them with wooden ones—with legs. But he should be remembered for his compassion, a rare quality in his day. The charity-hospital movement was largely due to his influence.

An even more radical protestant was John Hooper, who became Bishop of Gloucester and Worcester in 1550.

Whereas Ridley crusaded against stone altars, Hooper inveighed against popish vestments. In his case too the trivial facts tend to crowd out the important ones from the history books. The important fact about Hooper was his revival of the pastoral concept of the office and work of a bishop.

Some sweeping changes were decreed by Edward's first Parliament. These included the abolition of many traditional objects and practices in worship, such as the ringing of bells at mass. But it should be noted that a law was passed aimed at curbing a certain kind of protestant extremism by making it unlawful to ridicule the eucharist.

Liturgical reform

It is natural for Anglicans especially, at the mention of Edward VI, to think at once of "the first and second Prayer Books of Edward VI." These were not actually "of" the boy king at all, but of Thomas Cranmer. In the midst of the surging theological and political revolution Cranmer was quietly working out his plan to supersede the Roman service books with an English liturgy. He was by no means the originator of liturgical reform; in fact, Cranmer's liturgical genius was not that of the originator but that of the editor, compiler, translator and adapter. Cranmer made use of traditional Latin materials as he had received them, and borrowed heavily from two contemporary liturgical reformers: the Spanish Cardinal Quignon, whose reformed breviary appeared in 1535, and the German Lutheran Hermann's *Consultations*.

Under Henry there had been some steps toward liturgical reform, but the first major change came in the first year of Edward's reign in the form of a royal injunction requiring some liturgical changes. The next year, Parliament ordered the administration of the holy communion in both kinds to the laity, and an appropriate order for this practice was issued by royal proclamation. This order supplemented the

Latin mass, which was kept intact. It was provided that at
the time of the people's communion the priest should ad-
dress the people briefly in English. Then followed, in practically their present form, what Anglicans call the general
confession and absolution, comfortable words (Scriptural
passages giving assurance of God's forgiveness), and the
prayer of humble access (a supplication as one approaches
the altar to receive the divine gift). It was provided that the
communicants were to receive first the bread and then the
wine. The priest administering was to say: "The body of our
Lord Jesus Christ, which was given for thee" (administering the chalice, "The blood of our Lord Jesus Christ, which
was shed for thee") "preserve thy body and soul unto everlasting life." The service was to close with an English blessing. This "Order of the Communion" was for interim use,
until a complete new English service was ready.

Although Cranmer is commonly regarded as the author
of the Book of Common Prayer, two qualifications need to
be made. First, he had several collaborators, about whom
we know very little except that they did work with him as
consultants. The other, as noted above, is that he was primarily an editor. Most of what comes from his pen in the
Prayer Book was originally the work of others, drawn from
traditional liturgical sources. This is true, for example, of
most of the collects for Sundays and holy days. But whatever Cranmer touched became stylistically his own, and
went forth transformed, usually for the better.

Cranmer's first Prayer Book appeared in 1549. In preparing his choir offices for the use of all people, which came
to be known as Matins (Morning Prayer) and Evensong
(Evening Prayer), he took the traditional monastic offices
as his working material. His scheme for the daily offices provides that the Psalter will be read through entirely each
month and that a large part of the Bible will be covered
each year in the appointed lections.

The eucharist in the 1549 Book is captioned "The Supper
of the Lorde and the Holy Communion, commonly called

the Masse." The service is based on the Sarum Missal, which was the medieval English adaptation of the Latin rite. It was much too conservative a revision to satisfy the radical protestants, despite the changes in theological implication and emphasis which Cranmer worked into it. In this 1549 rite he tried to eliminate all suggestions that the eucharist is a sacrifice which supplements or repeats the sacrifice on Calvary. In it only one sacrifice is pleaded—that of Christ on the Cross, "who made there (by his one oblation once offered) a full, perfect, and sufficient sacrifice, oblation, and satisfaction, for the sins of the whole world." Most conservative, catholic-minded people found this rite acceptable. Its only radical novelty was being in English. As a spectacle, the mass was still the mass: the traditional alb, cope, and other vestments were retained. The canon contained supplications for the dead. The Blessed Virgin and other saints were commemorated, though not invoked. Auricular confession was retained, but no longer required. Anointing was omitted at confirmation but retained in baptism and in the visitation of the sick.

As the prototype of all subsequent Anglican liturgy, the 1549 Prayer Book was an immortal achievement, but few if any at the time saw it as such. As a national irenicon, designed to promote religious unity, it was a failure. The parish clergy as a whole seem to have received it fairly well, having by this time become accustomed to government dictation. (The Prayer Book was imposed by royal decree.) The common folk in western England, especially in Devon and Cornwall, resisted it violently. Having the service in English was no help to them, since their common tongue was not English but a dialect of Welsh.

Cranmer patiently undertook a revision, hoping next time to please everybody or as many as possible. Along with most of the nation he was moving rapidly in a protestant direction, and his second Prayer Book, that of 1552, reflects this. From the 1552 book were removed all traces of the idea that the eucharistic sacrifice is offered for the living and the dead.

There was an almost total abolition of verbal or ceremonial recognition of the real presence of Christ on the altar. Also omitted were prayers for the dead, anointing of the sick, and exorcism in baptism. The 1552 book was acceptable to all but the most extreme protestants. It was officially put into use on November 1, 1552, but it was to have a short life that would end with the death of Edward the following summer.

"Ill fares the land"

The religious troubles of the realm were accompanied by social and economic troubles, and their brunt fell upon Somerset. Among his foes was his own brother, Thomas Seymour, Lord High Admiral. Thomas had married Catherine Parr, widow of Henry VIII, and Princess Elizabeth was living with them. The admiral conspired against the government headed by his brother, was caught, and executed; but this was the beginning of woes for Somerset.

The lot of the rural poor had grown desperate with the economic revolution. Something has already been said about the enclosures of land. Fields which formerly had yielded food for the poor now yielded food for the sheep of the rich. In some counties as much as a third of the arable land was enclosed. The new nobility which owned most of it had got much of the money to buy up the land by looting churches and monasteries. For this reason the angry commoners associated their economic plight with the religious revolution. Somerset tried hard to redress such wrongs, but could not. His hands were tied by the fact that so many men in his government were themselves greedy profiteers who had helped to create the wrong. In 1549 a serious revolt, Ket's rebellion, broke out in Norfolk. Its leader, Robert Ket, was a tannery owner. Some sixteen thousand peasants joined his camp outside Norwich. There, under an oak, Ket sat in judgment upon the robbers of the poor. These rebels shed no blood, but lived upon the flocks and herds of the land-owners. The local authorities could not cope with them.

Lord Somerset himself declared publicly his belief in the justice of the cause of the rebels, and this was the pretext desired by his arch enemy, John Dudley, Earl of Warwick. Troops under Warwick's command were sent to suppress the uprising, and the rebels were routed and slaughtered. Warwick was now the hero of the rich and influential, and Somerset the scapegoat. In October 1549 Somerset was deposed, and Warwick succeeded him as Lord Protector. (Warwick is generally remembered in history as Northumberland. He was made Duke of Northumberland in 1551.)

The Northumberland protectorate (1549–53) was a time of misery for most English folk. The land was ruled by and for landlords, most of whom were newly rich and insatiably greedy. Parliament was their compliant tool and enacted laws savagely punishing the peasants. Northumberland allied himself with the more radical protestant reformers because with them apparently went the wave of the future. It was a bad day for the cause of the English reformation when Northumberland and his cronies hypocritically embraced its cause, and rendered lip service to it.

Edward died in July 1553. At once Northumberland tried to seize Princess Mary, the daughter of Henry by Catherine, to prevent her accession, but she escaped. He now tried the desperate device that involved Lady Jane Grey. She was a grandchild of a union between Henry VII's younger daughter and the Duke of Suffolk. Henry VIII had named the heirs of this union next in line of succession after his own children. Lady Jane, now 16, was the oldest child of this family; and Northumberland, to get her under his control, had married her to his own son Guildford Dudley. He planned to stage a military *coup* at Edward's death and to put his daughter-in-law on the throne. But he had badly misjudged public opinion. He and all his works were detested throughout the land. Poor Lady Jane did not want to

be queen anyway. Eventually she would have to die a victim
of the designs of others who, for their own reasons, wanted
her to be queen.

The nation rejoiced when it learned that Mary Tudor
would be its next queen, not out of love for her but out of
hatred for Northumberland. He had sworn that his only
concern was for the true protestant religion, but the English
reformation had been foully betrayed by this "friend." The
nation was in a mood to consider a return to the old religious *status pro ante*. The so-called reformation had
brought no liberation from religious tyranny. The burdens
of the poor had not been lightened but cruelly augmented.
There was no peace. Everybody hoped, therefore, that
Princess Mary, who had suffered more than twenty years of
humiliation, would be a gentle, just, and godly queen.

Chapter Twelve

Counter-Revolution

I cannot tell how naturally the mother loveth her child, for I
was never the mother of any; but certainly if a queen may as
naturally and earnestly love her subjects as the mother doth her
child, then assure yourselves that I, being your lady and mistress,
do as earnestly and tenderly love and favor you.
Mary Tudor, Queen of England, to her subjects, after a conspiracy against her in 1554.

The new queen began her reign with a firm resolve to
reconcile her political enemies and religious adversaries. She
had spent the 38 years of her life for the most part in loneli-
ness and sadness, but she was not bitter or revengeful. There
was hope for a happier future in her heart as she rode to
London amidst the cheers of her new subjects. That hope,
however, would die young.

In a proclamation early in her reign Mary declared her
allegiance to Roman Catholicism but added that until further notice there would be no change in the religious situation. She intended to make all changes legally, peaceably,
and in such a way as to make it possible for all subjects of
good will to adjust to them. Quite evidently she had no idea
of the nature and extent of the anti-Roman revolution that
had taken place. She believed that the nation as a whole
could be restored to Rome by law and by persuasion.

Five conservative bishops who had been deprived under

Edward were restored. Among these was Stephen Gardiner, Bishop of Winchester, who was now made Lord Chancellor. Gardiner presided at the session of Parliament in the fall of 1554 at which the Act of Uniformity of 1552, which had required conformity to the Prayer Book, was repealed. It was further enacted that on December 20th of that year all Prayer Book services must cease, and that the Latin services which had been in use in the last year of Henry's reign should be restored. Thus far the queen carried Parliament with her. The lack of resistence convinced her that England was ready to repudiate the whole of the Reformation. Here she miscalculated badly. There was a general willingness to return to the non-papal catholicism of Henry in his last days, but it was not a willingness to return to the papal obedience.

The queen made three major mistakes. One was her marriage to Prince Philip of Spain. The second was her choice of Reginald Cardinal Pole to succeed Cranmer as Archbishop of Canterbury. The third was her decision to try to coerce the nation to go all the way back to the Roman order.

When she married Philip in 1555 she was 38 and he was ten years younger. Bishop Gardiner and other government leaders implored her not to marry the Spaniard, since nothing could more thoroughly alienate the English people. The popular fear was that England would become a tool of Spanish imperial politics. Spain and France were the main adversaries in Europe; if England became a Spanish vassal state through this royal union it would be forced into enmity with France. Most Englishmen were hardly pro-French, but they were decidedly anti-Spanish. The nation so resented this marriage that the city of Plymouth actually asked the King of France to take it under his protection, and open revolt broke out in four counties. An army of seven thousand, led by Sir Thomas Wyatt the Younger, marched toward London. This was civil war. Wyatt's rebellion was put down, but it caused a change in Mary's attitude and policy toward her opponents. She concluded that she had been too slow to punish and too quick to pardon. Henceforth she would be ruthless.

In November 1554 Cardinal Pole arrived as papal legate. He was an Englishman of noble blood, in fact a second cousin to the queen. His family had suffered much at the hands of Henry VIII and Pole had grown up abroad in exile. He returned to England with no base desire for revenge or self-enrichment. His only business was to restore England to the papal obedience. He came from Rome with a reasonable and conciliatory program. The pope had decided not to demand the restoration to the Church of any of the confiscated treasures and property. There was to be pardon and amnesty for all who, having rebelled against the papal rule and order, were now willing to submit. The pope's ecclesiastical supremacy was re-established, the payment of annates and "first fruits" to Rome was resumed, the church courts were revived, the payment of tithes to the clergy was restored. In sum, the clock was turned back about twenty years; or rather, the effort was made. The queen and the cardinal failed to see the impossibility of this retrogression.

Something had happened during these twenty years which passed their comprehension. It cannot be called the triumph of protestantism in the English soul. It wasn't so much the growth of some new things as it was the desuetude of some old things. There had grown up a general scepticism about the rightness and soundness of that old religious order which Mary wanted to restore. There were proliferating new, shocking ideas in religion, some of these born of hatred of Rome. Mary was astonished and horrified to learn that among her subjects were some who denied Christ's divinity, some who denied the existence of the Holy Ghost, some who denied the transmission of original sin. Pamphlets were circulated in which the "lousy Latin service" was called the "idolatrous mass." Both queen and cardinal were devotees of the sort who can view heresy only with horror. They had hoped that the heretics would respond happily, or at least sensibly, to their leniency. When they realized that this hope was vain they turned to persecution as a policy.

The reign of terror began early in 1555. First, heretical clergymen, then laymen—many of these being simple workingmen who had learned to read the Bible—were hailed into episcopal court. Each was given opportunity to recant. Failure to do so meant death at the stake. In February John Hooper, deposed Bishop of Gloucester and Worcester, died in the flames. In September came the trials of the most famous martyrs: Cranmer, who was 66, Ridley, 65, and Latimer, 80. Cranmer had been the intellectual leader of the English reformation. He had dissolved the marriage of Henry and Catharine, married Henry to Anne Boleyn, composed the Book of Common Prayer, signed the document by which Edward devised the crown to Jane Grey, and called the mass a blasphemy. Latimer had approved the burning of some Franciscans under Henry VIII and had preached against the pope. Ridley had actively supported the plot to put Jane Grey on the throne, and had called Mary a bastard. Latimer and Ridley were burned on October 6th, and as the faggots were lighted Latimer spoke the words which will be remembered forever in England: "Be of good cheer, Master Ridley, and play the man; we shall this day light such a candle, by God's grace, in England as I trust shall never be put out." Cranmer, confronted by a hard choice between recanting and dying at the stake, faltered for a moment; but when he came to die, on March 21, 1556, he died in the manner of St. Stephen the Martyr, crying "Lord Jesus, receive my spirit."

Some three hundred persons died for their faith under Mary. The experience of persecution gave the protestants a cohesion they had lacked before. The English people reacted very positively against the queen's policy of persecution. It was not because they disapproved of killing dissenters from the legally prescribed religion: under Henry and Edward there had been such penalties, and under Elizabeth there would be more. Capital punishment by burning was not unusual or abhorrent. Although several hundred were executed, this was no great holocaust when judged by massacres and mass executions on the continent. Why then did the nation reproach and condemn its queen as Bloody Mary? There seem to be several reasons. One is that most Englishmen did not share the feeling of the queen and the cardinal that the very presence on earth of a live heretic was an outrage to God and a menace to man. There was lacking a national mood of passionate dogmatic triumphalism. There was lacking also a strong sense of urgent *national* peril in face of the protestant movement. Some thirty years later, when England would be haunted by the Spanish menace, the English would be quite willing to burn any priest who might be suspected of being an agent of Spain and the pope.

In a recent study of the Reformation in England A. G. Dickens summarizes the effect of the Marian persecutions thus:

The madness of a system which would burn a virtuous human being for his inability to accept a metaphysical theory of the Eucharist must stagger even a generation well accustomed to institutional and doctrinaire crimes. Moreover, many a modern observer would hesitate to attribute mental balance to a man who suffered himself to be burned over such an uncertainty. Yet the Marian reaction did at least reveal a wealth of human fortitude, of "civil courage," of adherence to mere principle which the English have seldom in their history found a comparable chance to display. For both good and ill it became an integral part of the memory of a people; it took its place alongside King Alfred, the Black Prince and Agincourt as a factor in the evolution of our national self-consciousness. By every right it was a story which belonged to the common man, and slowly, indirectly, deviously, it helped to supply some of the elements of constitutional and social libertarianism. Though the contestants of the seventeenth century understood the nature of liberty better than those of the sixteenth, the later stage could scarcely have arrived save on the basis of the former. Though the memory of the Marian martyrs provoked Protestant bigotry, it also helped to provoke more worthy and creative attitudes—an independence of outlook, a confidence that the future belongs to God—all those attitudes we find fully developed amid the contemporaries of Oliver Cromwell, John Milton and John Bunyan.[1]

It was not only the persecution of protestants that made the queen increasingly odious to her subjects. As many had feared, the royal alliance with Spain had dragged England into a disastrous war with France. England lost Calais, its last possession on the continent. Thousands of English people who had lived there had to flee, homeless and penniless and bitterly reproaching Mary's government for failing in their defense. The queen was blamed for this national humiliation.

Her failure to become pregnant drove Mary at last to brooding melancholy. In the fall of 1558 she was stricken with the ague fever, and died on November 17th. Cardinal Pole died on the same day. Together they had prayed and striven for the reconciliation of England to Rome. The result of all their striving was a breach wider and deeper than ever before.

[1] A. G. Dickens, *The English Reformation*, 271.

Chapter Thirteen

The Elizabethan Settlement

They talk much of settling Religion: Religion is well enough settled already, if we would let it alone.

John Selden Esq. (1584–1654)

The reign of Elizabeth I (1558–1603) was one of the decisive epochs for all English history. In religion it was the time of the final settlement in which Anglicanism emerged in the essential form it has had to this day.

The daughter of Henry VIII was like her father in political ability, boldness coupled with shrewdness, and personal popularity. She began her reign facing some grave difficulties and perils. England had never been ruled successfully by a woman, and the whole world had to be shown that it could be done. In the eyes of Roman Catholics she was illegitimate and therefore had no right to rule. The men in charge of the English Church at her accession had supported Mary and were pro-papal. The nation was in dire peril from enemies abroad. For thirty years, until the destruction of the Armada in 1588, England would know no secure international peace. The first foreign threat was that of the Franco-Scottish coalition aimed at Elizabeth. Fortunately, she had the support of Philip II of Spain in resisting this. He was resolved to prevent a possible union of France, England and Scotland under Mary "Queen of Scots" and her husband who in 1559 became King Francis II of France. From the standpoint of Spanish power politics a protestant ruler of an independent England was preferable to that. Later, Spain would become England's deadliest foe.

Because England's security was so precarious Elizabeth determined from the outset to have national unity based upon religious unity. If the Church of England would finally emerge as "the roomiest Church on Christendom" it was largely because only a very comprehensive Church could embrace the whole nation.

Elizabeth herself was a protestant, inevitably so because of her birth, upbringing, and whole situation. She was protestant in the sense that she was determined that the pope should not have his way with England. This was about her only agreement with the radical protestants. Her tastes in worship and beliefs were rather mixed. She liked the crucifix, vestments, and most of the traditional ceremonial, though she objected to the elevation of the host in the mass. She disliked a married clergy. She detested both protestant and catholic fanaticisms. In a word, she was naturally well fitted to the task of leading her people toward a religious settlement which would "settle" by virtue of its comprehensiveness. She was, for her age, religiously very tolerant.

She proceeded slowly and cautiously with the religious changes she thought necessary for reasons of state. The new Supremacy Act was passed in Parliament, over much opposition, in April 1559. It abolished the authority of the pope in England and outlawed all payments and appeals to him. Elizabeth insisted upon a change in the royal title from "Supreme Head" to "Supreme Governor" of the Church of England. While neither Henry nor Mary had exercised "headship" in any other than a legal or custodial sense, the title "Supreme Head" suggested a spiritual primacy that was unacceptable to most protestants as well as catholics. The jurist John Selden would state the distinction thus in the days of James I:

There is a great difference between the head of the Church and supreme governor, as our canons call the king . . . Conceive it

thus, there is in the Kingdom of England a college of physicians:
the King is supreme governor of those, but not head of them,
nor president of the college, nor the best physician.

Elizabeth saw the distinction in those terms. She claimed
no right to personal control over the Church's doctrine and
worship. Moreover, she saw Parliament as her partner and
not as her rubber-stamp.

Also in 1559, the Act of Uniformity re-established the
Prayer Book of 1552, with a few noteworthy changes. The
"Black Rubric" of 1552 was now omitted. This rubric had
explained that when communicants kneel to receive communion "it is not meant thereby that any adoration is done
or ought to be done, either unto the sacramental bread and
wine there bodily received, or to any real and essential presence there being of Christ's natural flesh and blood." This
had been intended as a denial and prohibition of belief in
the sacramental real presence of Christ. Its repeal in 1559
meant that Churchmen could in good conscience believe in
and adore Christ on the altar. Also at this time a classic
piece of liturgical comprehension was done with the words
used in administering the sacrament. In the 1549 Prayer
Book the prescribed sentence clearly implied Christ's sacramental presence: "The body of our Lord Jesus Christ, which
was given for thee, preserve thy body and soul unto everlasting life." The protestants rejected this, and in 1552 it
was replaced by a sentence implying that Christ's presence
is not in the sacrament but in the heart of the faithful receiver: "Take and eat this in remembrance that Christ died
for thee, and feed on him in thy heart, by faith, with thanksgiving." The 1549 sentence was "catholic," the 1552 sentence was "protestant." Now the two sentences were simply
combined. The sentences used in administering the chalice
were similarly dealt with, and so it has been from that day
to this.

Elizabeth's choice for Archbishop of Canterbury was the
capable Matthew Parker. By both conviction and tempera-
ment he was well equipped for the task of working out a

religious settlement that would be both catholic and reformed. But there was a problem in getting him consecrated.
The Marian bishops, *i.e.* those who had been chosen and
consecrated under Mary, were pro-papal and could not accept the new order, so they would have no part in conse-
crating Parker. There were, however, four bishops still living
who had been consecrated under Henry VIII or Edward VI.
On December 17, 1559 these four bishops consecrated
Matthew Parker. This made possible the establishment of a
whole new English episcopate deriving its orders from
Parker. But to this day Parker's consecration has been a bone
of contention between the Roman and Anglican Churches,
the former alleging, on various grounds, that Parker's consecration was not capable of validating Anglican orders deriving from it. It satisfied the queen and the English nation at
the time, however, and Anglicans ever since have been sure
of the integrity of the episcopal ministry of their Church.

Articles of religion

The 16th century was an age of "confessional" or de-
nominational statements of religious opinion. The Lutherans presented their Augsbury Confession, the Calvinists
their Westminister Confession, the Roman Catholics their
decrees of the Council of Trent, and the Anglicans their
Articles of Religion.

The Anglican Articles began in 1536 with the Ten
Articles, which Henry VIII helped to compose. Their declared object was "to establish Christian quietness and unity
among us and to avoid contentious opinions." These conservative and catholic Articles remained in force until 1543
when they were in effect superseded by a treatise commonly
known as *The King's Book*, a document which emphatically
affirms transubstantiation against the growing assault upon
that doctrine by the reformers. At Henry's death in 1547
Cranmer took over the task of article-making. In 1552 a

corpus of 42 Articles was submitted to the Council of Government, then returned to Cranmer for editing and abridging. These 42 Articles were issued in English in May 1553, but Edward died that summer and with Mary's accession the Articles were dropped. Under Elizabeth the 42 Articles were revived to serve as the basis of the later and permanent formulations. As polemic pieces the Articles attack two enemies: the revolutionary and anarchical anabaptists, and the "School-authors" or medieval scholastics. The Roman reply to the attack upon the "School-authors" would come from the Council of Trent (1545–1562).

Early in 1563 the Church Convocation was given the task of revising the Articles, but both Cranmer and Parker had done some article-framing of their own, and their efforts were made use of by Convocation. The purpose of the Articles was to set definite, but very broad, limits upon what men could believe as loyal members of the Church of England. The limits were so drawn as to exclude two kinds of religion, at opposite poles from each other: papal catholicism and anabaptism. These were the two forms of Christianity which had to be by their very nature opposed to the Elizabethan state. Papal catholicism would replace royal supremacy with papal supremacy, while the anabaptists would have *no* human "supremacy" at all, being absolute anarchists in principle.

Elizabeth began her reign accepting all subjects, whatever their religious views or allegiances, so long as they were loyal to the crown. Recusants—those who adhered to the papacy —were included. She hoped that some way of comprehending recusants within the national Church could be found, and during the first twelve years of her reign not one Roman Catholic was put to death for his faith. But the situation of promise was changed in February 1570, when Pope Pius V issued the bull *Regnans in Excelsis*. It declared that Elizabeth was a heretic with no right to the English throne, that her subjects were not bound by any oath of loyalty to her, and any Roman Catholic who remained obedient to her was liable to excommunication. Thus with a stroke of the pen the pope made every English Roman Catholic a traitor under the civil law.

In 1568, the pope tried to engineer an overthrow of Elizabeth's rule through Mary Queen of Scots. Many Englishmen regarded Mary rather than Elizabeth as the lawful heiress to the throne. In November 1569 the recusants in northern England openly rebelled with the object of driving Elizabeth from the throne and enthroning Mary. This rebellion was quickly put down, but it apparently gave Pope Pius V the idea that England was ready to rise against Elizabeth. She was "tried" in Rome (in her absence and without representation), found guilty, excommunicated and deposed. Her sentence was pronounced in *Regnans in Excelsis*. This miscalculated action by the pope destroyed any possibility of future reconciliation between Rome and England.

Having emerged from the Council of Trent in an aggressive mood, the Roman Church was counter-attacking protestantism and the recovery of England was a prime goal. In 1568 an English recusant, William Allen, founded the seminary at Douai in France. It was the first of several training centers for Roman Catholic missionaries to England. By 1580 there were more than a hundred of these men at work in England. They saw their task as that of winning people to papal catholicism, but the government saw them as enemy agents working for a foreign power which had openly declared its purpose to overthrow the government of the realm.

The government prosecuted these mission priests with unrelenting energy and with a severity that appalls us. Informers against them were employed, testimony was extracted by torture, and the court procedures were often a travesty. All this is indefensible but quite easily explainable: the explanation is fear. England was in a state of constant grave danger from 1570 to 1590. It was only in the last years of Elizabeth's reign, after the defeat of the Armada in 1588, that the nation could feel reasonably secure against foreign

foes, and when it arrived at this stage the persecution of the
Romanists was abated. Elizabeth's conflict with the Roman
Church was political. As she saw it, and as in fact it was with
respect to her reign, it was a foreign and hostile power. Its
martyrs under Elizabeth were executed not for heresy but
for treason.

Puritanism

The people who came to be known as the puritans were
the more radical protestants who were not satisfied with the
reformation of the Church under Elizabeth. They demanded a complete "purification," by which they meant the
removal of all forms and ceremonies which they regarded
as unscriptural.

The puritans had several distinct aims, which they pur-
sued with uncompromising zeal. One aim was a purely
preaching ministry, and preaching to them meant expound-
ing the Scriptures. Another aim was the abolition of all forms
and ceremonies not explicitly enjoined in the Scriptures;
hence their condemnation of such things as the sign of the
cross in baptism and the wearing of the surplice. Another
puritan aim was to replace the whole traditional episcopal
structure of the Church with presbyterianism after the pattern of Geneva. Such a change would mean the abolition of
bishops, the equality or parity of all ministers, establishment
of parish consistories with disciplinary power over parishioners, and lay participation in church government.

Puritanism was subversive in Elizabethan England because the queen's policy called for a national unity based
upon the religious unity provided by the Church of England,
and the puritans could not accept the Church as it was. Because conformity to the Prayer Book was required by law
they were driven underground, and met secretly to worship.
These secret meetings for Bible study and prayer usually
took place on weekday mornings and came to be known as

"prophesyings." To us they may seem to have been harmless at worst. The trouble was that they threatened to replace the rites of the Church. Elizabeth regarded them as disloyal and subversive. In 1577 she urged the bishops to suppress the prophesyings. Little came of it, however. There was a tough vitality in English puritanism, and it grew apace.

From Elizabeth's point of view, puritanism was the enemy working from within the Church of England, while Romanism was the enemy working from without, and about both she was right. These two resolute and powerful forces had one thing in common: their desire to frustrate and to defeat that ordering of the nation's religion which was the Elizabethan Settlement.

Chapter Fourteen

The Via Media

Our reformation was done without tumult, and yet we saw it necessary to reform; we were zealous to cast away the old errors, but our zeal was balanced with consideration and the results of authority: not like women or children when they are affrighted with fire in their clothes, we shaked off the coal indeed, but not our garments, lest we should have exposed our churches to that nakedness which the excellent men of our sister Churches complained to be among themselves.

Jeremy Taylor (1613–67)

The statement that the English reformation was an act of state is quite accurate, for reasons which have been touched upon in the last four chapers. We have traced the political course of events rather closely. It is now time to review the changes in doctrine, polity, and worship in the English Church, such as they were, which resulted from that Church's parting of the ways with Rome and the impact of the manifold protestant movement upon it.

Anglicanism is commonly described as the *Via Media*. It is an appropriate label but it needs careful and precise definition. "The middle way" is an inaccurate and misleading English equivalent, while "the middle of the road way" is worse. All who live in the motor age should know that the worst possible way to drive a car is in the middle of the road rather than well over in the right lane. Another familiar

label for Anglicanism whose overtones are not entirely
felicitous is "the bridge Church." This is meant to suggest
that Anglicanism provides a bridge between catholicism and
protestantism since it is grounded in both shores. But a
bridge is no place to live, and souls do live and thrive in this
"bridge" Church.

The term "middle way" as a translation of *Via Media* is
literally correct, but in modern idiom it suggests some kind
of half-way house. The Anglicans who first spoke of the
Via Media had in mind not a compromise but a comprehending, reconciling, mediating way between historic catholicism and the renewing elements in the Reformation.
In the last chapter we noted what might be taken as an example of the *via median* way of the English reformers. In the
1549 Prayer Book the sentence of administration at the communion of the people was "catholic" in expressing an awareness that Christ is present in the sacrament: "The body of
our Lord Jesus Christ, which was given for thee, preserve
thy body and soul unto everlasting life." The sentence
which replaced that one in the 1552 book was "protestant"
in implying that Christ must be present in the heart and
will of the faithful receiver: "Take and eat this in remembrance that Christ died for thee, and feed on him in thy
heart, by faith, with thanksgiving." In the final Anglican
resolution of the issue the two sentences were combined.
The *via median* principle is that both of these are essential
truths about Christ's presence in holy communion which are
not contradictory but complementary, and so they must be
given a comprehending and reconciling—i.e. *via median*—
expression.

For Anglicanism the *Via Media* represents another essential quality. The English reformers saw that, although
the Church of their fathers had faithfully received and
taught the essentials of the Gospel, it had also picked up
many non-essentials in its journey through the centuries.
They were determined to preserve the essentials and to

abolish—or make optional—the non-essentials. Cranmer in his liturgical work was primarily motivated by this purpose. The reformers usually expressed the distinction as being between "things necessary for salvation" and "things convenient in practice." There developed a solid Anglican consensus about the things necessary. The essential *credenda* were contained in the Apostles' and Nicene Creeds; the sacraments necessary to salvation were baptism and the eucharist. Upon these fundamental *credenda* and *agenda* the Church must insist; as for the "things convenient in practice"—edifying doctrines, rites, and ceremonies—it might provide whatever it felt guided at any given time to provide.

Such were the primary implications of the *Via Media* in the minds of its molders and shapers.

The Elizabethan Act of Uniformity declared that "heresy" is any doctrine that has been proscribed as heresy by any of the first four general councils of the Church, or any doctrine contrary to the canonical Scriptures, or any doctrine which might be condemned by any church council on the basis of the authority of the Scriptures. Here it is clear that the Bible is being made the "rule" or authoritative determiner and criterion of essential doctrine. It is declared in the 8th Article of Religion that the Apostles', Nicene, and Athanasian Creeds are received, "for they may be proved by most certain warrants of Holy Scripture." In the 20th Article it is laid down that although

the Church hath power to decree Rites or Ceremonies, and authority in Controversies of Faith" it is "not lawful for the Church to ordain any thing that is contrary to God's Word written . . . .

The Church is "a witness and a keeper of Holy Writ."

In Article 25 the sacraments are carefully defined along *via median* lines. Zwingli's conception of the sacraments as merely symbolic is excluded by the statement that they be not only badges or tokens of Christian men's profession, but rather they be certain and sure witnesses, and effectual signs of grace and God's good will towards us, by the which He doth work invisibly in us, and doth not only quicken, but also strengthen and confirm our Faith in Him.

In Article 28 the Lord's Supper is declared to be

a Sacrament of our Redemption by Christ's death; insomuch that to such as rightly, worthily, and with faith receive the same, the Bread which we break is a partaking of the Body of Christ, and likewise the Cup of blessing is a partaking of the Blood of Christ.

The Article rejects transubstantiation and affirms that

the Body of Christ is given, taken, and eaten in the Supper only after an heavenly and spiritual manner; and the mean whereby the Body of Christ is received and eaten in the Supper is Faith.

The eucharistic doctrine of Article 25 would be given fuller expression in a section on the sacraments added to the Prayer Book catechism in 1604. The catechism teaches that the eucharist was ordained "for the continual remembrance of the sacrifice of the death of Christ and of the benefits which we receive thereby"; the outward part, or sign, is "bread and wine," while the inward part, or thing signified, is "the Body and Blood of Christ which are verily and indeed taken and received by the faithful in the Lord's Supper"; the virtue, or benefit, of the eucharist is "the strengthening and refreshing of our souls by the Body and Blood of Christ as our bodies are by the bread and wine."

Sacramental doctrine concerning the eucharist was much more in controversy in England than was the doctrine of holy baptism, but it was affirmed, in Article 27, *contra* Zwingli, that "baptism is not only a sign of profession, and mark of difference" in Christian men, but an "instrument" of "Regeneration or New-Birth, whereby . . . they that receive Baptism rightly are grafted into the Church."

It is hard for the 20th-century student of the 16th-century

controversies over "justification" to follow most of the then
blazing polemics. The same is true of the heat that was gen-
erated in that age by such terms as predestination, election,
and free-will. What emerged as the Anglican position on
these issues is to be found in the Articles, some of it in language of baffling ambiguity. Articles 11 and 12 put forth the
position that man is justified—"accounted righteous before
God"—only by Christ's merits appropriated by faith, not by
his own "works or deservings"; yet those good works which
are the fruits of faith are "pleasing and acceptable to God
in Christ." The Lutheran phrase *sola fide*—"by faith alone"
is adopted, but in order to contradict the late medieval quasi-
Pelagian doctrine that a man can assure his own salvation
by good works. In Articles 9 and 17 a *via median* position is
expressed concerning predestination and election. It is affirmed that man "is very far gone from original righteousness," but this statement stops short, and with a purpose, of
the Calvinist dogma of universal total depravity.

Apologetics

Anglican apologetics begins with two eminent Elizabethan divines: John Jewel, Bishop of Salisbury, and his
pupil, Richard Hooker.

Jewel's defense of Anglicanism began with a sermon in
November 1559, in which he invoked the Scriptures and the
early Church in his thesis that the Church of England was
fully and truly catholic. This thesis he elaborated in his
treatise known as the *Apology*. The argument of Jewel's
Apology is that the real "innovators" are not the Anglicans
but the Romanists. Papal supremacy, it is argued, does not
meet the catholic test of antiquity, and must therefore be
regarded as an innovation. To reject this innovation is not
to fall into heresy and schism. The papacy is not part of the
Gospel, nor is it to be found in the original constitution of

the Church of the Scriptures, the apostles, and the fathers. Such in essence is Jewel's case against Rome and it remains to this day the Anglican answer to the papal claims. The appeal to Scriptures and to antiquity is normal and normative in Anglican apologetics.

Anglicanism has never had a Luther, or Calvin, or any such system-maker. No Anglican theologian needs to "swear by the word of the master," for there is no such master. But there is Richard Hooker (1554–1600), whose place in Anglicanism is like that of John of Damascus in Eastern Orthodoxy. Neither man was an innovator or systematizer. Each gave classic expression and formulation to what his Church taught—and was.

Both spiritually and intellectually Hooker towered above his age. Felix R. Arnott gives this just assessment of the nature of his influence:

Hooker succeeded in rescuing theological controversy from the filth of the market place, and investing it with a new and dignified splendor. When we pass from the scurrility of the Marprelate Tracts to Hooker's breadth of religious vision, we find ourselves in an altogether different *milieu*, where bickering about *minutiae* has given place to the reasoned examination of principles. In his writings we can trace the germ of the characteristic Anglican doctrine of *aurea mediocritas* laid down against the claims of both Rome and Geneva. Hallam justly described his *Ecclesiastical Polity* as the first great original prose work in our language, pointing out that its author "not only opened the mine, but explored the depths of our national eloquence." The *Polity* formed the stylistic basis on which most of the later divines built, and its long and straightforward periods are constantly re-echoed in the magnificent language of the Authorized Translation of the Bible. Hooker's spirit permeated almost all that was best in subsequent English religious thought, and his ideas were worked out to their full conclusions by Andrewes, Laud and Sanderson; for it was his task *serere arbores, quae alteri saeculo prosint.*[1]

Jewel had laid down the lines of Anglican apologetic

against Rome. Hooker addressed himself to answering the
puritan polemics. He was not, however, primarily a contro-
versialist. His *Polity* was intended as a platform of peace on
which all Christian men could stand united. He was reverently mindful of the wisest man's inability to comprehend
God and the eternal mysteries. The mind that speaks
through all his work is revealed in his often quoted statement
on the presence of Christ in the eucharist:

What these elements are in themselves it skilleth not, it is
enough that to me which take them they are the body and blood
of Christ, his promise in witness hereof sufficeth, his word he
knoweth which way to accomplish, why should any cogitation
possess the mind of a faithful communicant but this, "O my
God thou art true, O my Soul thou art happy!"

The puritans held that no rite or ceremony is lawful unless
explicitly enjoined by the Scriptures. Hooker argued in reply
that the Church may make its own laws and ordain its own
ceremonies so long as these are not contrary to Scripture.
He powerfully championed human reason without falling
into rationalism. His appeal was to experience, and to the
reliability of man's power to know God's truth when the
mind is humbly surrendered to the Holy Spirit. He declared
that nothing is to be rejected simply because the Romanists
have held it. On the fundamentals of the Christian faith—
the Holy Trinity, Christ's incarnation, atonement and resur-
rection—Hooker is unimpeachably catholic and orthodox.
His sacramental doctrine is less definite. He teaches that
baptism and the eucharist are real means of grace, but he
stresses that their salvific power lies not in the sacraments
themselves but comes from God. Concerning the eucharistic
real presence of Christ he reasoned that both transubstantiation and the Lutheran consubstantiation were inadequate
to express the mystery. He never did in fact come forth with
a positive doctrine of the real presence, for he felt that it is
both unnecessary and presumptuous to try to explain pre-

cisely what Christ does when in this sacrament he gives himself to his faithful people.

Hooker comes close to Calvin's doctrine in some of his statements about grace and election, but in all that he says about this he is chiefly concerned to say that a man can be saved only by the grace of Christ and never by his own merit. He does not teach Calvin's doctrine of double predestination, according to which God predestines some to damnation and others to salvation.

One of Hooker's primary premises is now totally obsolete. As an advocate of the Elizabethan Settlement he pleaded the cause of the national Church ruled by the Christian prince. In his age this made good sense; and since his time the Anglican establishment has been the instrument of many blessings to the English nation. But it has been a strictly temporal and local arrangement between Church and State, and many, perhaps most, English Churchmen today would like to see the relationship ended. It is only in England, and nowhere else within the Anglican Communion, that the Church is the official Church of the land. National church establishment has never been a peculiarly Anglican principle. Roman Catholic, Lutheran, and other Churches have been similarly "established" in countries where this was desired: *e.g.* the Roman Church in Spain, the Lutheran in Norway, the Presbyterian in Scotland.

Hooker established a pattern to which Anglican theology always returns when at its best: a pattern of openness to the Holy Spirit, a willingness to be instructed, to move, to change, to welcome new truths—however inconvenient. He would have agreed with Herbert Spencer that "the profoundest of all infidelities is the fear that the truth will be bad." At the same time, he strengthened catholic traditionalism in the Church of England. The puritan wanted to abolish anything "popish" simply because it was "popish." This is why in the end the puritans had to find their spiritual home outside the Church. Hooker was for preserving any practice or tradition until it could be shown to be anti-scriptural or incompatible with the mind of Christ, and his way prevailed.

16th century summary

Richard Hooker died in 1600, while Queen Elizabeth died three years later. The end of the century saw the end of the revolution occasioned by the break with Rome. In the 16th century the English Church had done the following things.

It had preserved the catholic faith as this had been taught in the Scriptures, the Creeds, and the doctrinal decrees of the first four general councils.

It had restored to its original catholic status the Bible as the supreme arbiter of all matters of faith and conduct.

It had restored the catholic usage of the language of the people in worship.

It had restored the apostolic and original administration of the eucharist to the people in both the Bread and the Wine.

In the rites of confirmation and ordination it had restored the original practice of the laying on of hands by the bishop as the essential in the rite.

It tried to restore the catholic practice of regular communion by all the faithful.

It retained the three-fold order of the ministry in apostolic succession: bishops, priests, and deacons.

It retained the liturgical order of the Christian Year, with modifications and simplifications.

It repudiated the supremacy of the pope.

It denied the authority of the pope to interfere in the civil affairs of the nation.

It claimed liberty for national Churches, within the fellowship of Christ's Holy Catholic Church, "to decree Rites or Ceremonies" (Article 20).

It rejected the claim that the medieval scholastic philosophy was the only fitting and proper one for Christian thinkers.

It rejected the medieval ideas of purgatory, indulgences, and the merits of the saints.

It retained, one must probably have to say unfortunately, the medieval ideas of property, jurisdiction, and ecclesiastical administration.

It claimed to be a living part of the worldwide Church of Christ.[2]

[1] In More and Cross, *Anglicanism*, xliv.
[2] In this summary I have followed very closely the summary Stephen Neill gives in his admirable book, *Anglicanism*, 131.

Chapter Fifteen

The King Supreme

The state of monarchy is the supremest thing on earth; for kings are not only God's lieutenants on earth, but even by God himself they are called gods.

James I

What speaks in these words of the first Stuart monarch is no mere psychopathic egomania but the doctrine that came to be known, and defended by some of England's finest Christian minds, as the Divine Right of Kings.

The Stuart kings lacked one thing that was strong in their Tudor predecessors: a sense of mystic unity with the English people. Henry and Elizabeth had been despotic and absolutist in both theory and practice; yet most Englishmen had felt that they were somehow their own. They had belonged to the people. The Stuarts felt that the people belonged to them.

When James mounted the throne in 1603 he brought the doctrine of Divine Right of Kings with him. He had been raised in Scotland under rigidly Calvinist tutors, but he sensed that the political principle implicit in Calvinism was opposed to monarchy so he would have none of it.

The England which he came to rule was deeply and dangerously at schism within itself. There were still thousands of recusants, and although a small minority they were numerous enough and dedicated enough to pose a continuing grave threat to the Anglican state. At the outset James felt that they needed close watching, but not active persecution. On the other flank were the puritans, much more numerous and openly active and aggressive. They had high hopes that James, with his Calvinist upbringing, would prove to be their man. They were unhappy with both Prayer Book and episcopacy, each of which in its own way curbed them. Moreover, puritanism was allied with the rising new middle class, represented by country squires and city merchants, who saw absolute monarchy as an anachronism and were bent upon increasing the power of Parliament, especially the House of Commons.

The hopeful puritans presented James with their Millenary Petition, subscribed to by a thousand clergy, while he was on his way south from Scotland. In it they set forth their grievances, demanding abolition of such things as the sign of the cross in baptism, wearing the surplice, bowing at the name of Jesus, and reading the apocryphal Scriptures in church. The king heard these complaints and requests at Hampton Court in 1604. A few concessions were made to the puritans, among them the promise of a new translation of the Bible; but in effect James declared war on them. "I have lived among this sort of men ever since I was ten years old," he said, "but I may say of myself, as Christ did of Himself, though I lived amongst them, I was never one of them." If they had their way, he remarked, "I know what would become of my supremacy. No bishop, no king. When I mean to live under a presbytery, I will go into Scotland again, but while I am in England, I will have bishops to govern the Church." "No bishop, no king": episcopacy was the ecclesiastical support and stay of monarchy. James's espousal of episcopacy would give it a momentary advantage, but later in the century bishop and king would go down together. In his moment of triumphalism he said of the puritans: "I will make them conform themselves or I will harry them out of this land or worse."

The Authorized Version

One great blessing came out of the Hampton Court conference: the English Bible variously known as the Authorized Version and the King James Version. Both these titles are misnomers. This Bible was never "authorized" by ecclesiastical authority for use in the Church; it was simply "appointed to be read." The term "King James Version" suggests that it was the king's own work, which it was not. He is entitled to credit, however, for the impulse he gave to the project.

The translation was done by six committees, numbering about 50 in all, from 1604 to 1611.[1] Gustavus S. Paine well describes these men as "minor writers, though great scholars, doing superb writing."[2] Among the many glowing tributes to the beauty and felicity of the AV as literature which Mr. Paine quotes in his book, this one by the late Henry L. Mencken is typical, and especially weighty because it comes from so thoroughly "unecclesiastical" a critic: "It is the most beautiful of all the translations of the Bible," Mencken wrote.

Indeed, it is probably the most beautiful piece of writing in all the literature of the world. Many attempts have been made to purge it of its errors and obscurities. An English Revised Version was published in 1885 and an American Revised Version in 1901, and since then many learned but misguided men have sought to produce translations that should be mathematically accurate, and in the plain speech of everyday. But the Authorized Version has never yielded to any of them, for it is palpably and overwhelmingly better than they are, just as it is better than the Greek New Testament, or the Vulgate, or the Septuagint. Its English is extraordinarily simple, pure, eloquent, and lovely. It is a mine of lordly and incomparable poetry, at once the most stirring and the most touching ever heard of.

Since Mencken wrote these words a generation ago there has been much fruitful work done in Bible translation. Present-day scholars have better Greek and Hebrew texts to work with than did King James's men. But the task of improving upon the Authorized Version, like that of improving upon Cranmer's Prayer Book, baffles and frustrates all comers. The effect of these two books in their original classic texts upon not only the worship but the very life and soul of Anglicans is deep, irreplaceable, and beyond all calculation or analysis.

Growing conflict

James was tolerant of the recusants at first, but in 1605 the Gunpowder Plot was uncovered. The English Romanists had hoped that once Elizabeth was dead and James was on the throne the pope would mollify his position and would allow them to give secular allegiance to their king, and that the king in turn would give them full religious freedom. The pope made no such concession. This plunged some recusants into despair, out of which developed the Gunpowder Plot. The plotters were some fanatics who planned to blow up the parliament building while king, lords, and commons were in session. A wave of hatred of Roman Catholics swept over the nation, and the penal laws against them were stiffened in their enforcement.

As "Supreme Governor" of the Church James saw himself as the theological schoolmaster of the realm. Along with this he claimed the right to bestow choice clerical offices upon his favorites, and exercised it in such a way that the Church became a royally controlled bureaucracy. A sad deterioration in the quality of the episcopate inevitably followed. Time-servers and sycophants rose to the purple, and John Milton was not being groundlessly scurrilous when he railed against "swan-eating, canary-sucking bishops." The bishops of James's age were primarily politicians rather than spiritual fathers, and unwittingly they helped to bring on a day of fearful reckoning for the Church.

There were, however, some noble exceptions among the bishops and clergy. Two in particular call for special notice. The first is Lancelot Andrewes (1555–1626), Bishop successively of Chichester, Ely and Winchester. Andrewes was one of England's finest saints of all time. His contemporary Robert Fuller noted that "his gravity in manner awed King James, who refrained from that mirth and liberty in the presence of this prelate which he otherwise assumed to himself." What the king encountered in Andrewes was not humorlessness but holiness. Theologically, Andrewes was in the Hooker pattern and tradition. He was vastly learned, especially in languages, and served as chairman of the translators of the Authorized Version. In liturgical matters he was one of the first of the great High Church divines, but he had no itch to impose his tastes and opinions upon others.

The other luminary of the age was John Donne (1573–1631), Dean of St. Paul's. He had been raised a Roman Catholic. His conversion to Anglicanism was deep and passionately earnest, yet he never became an ardent polemicist against Rome. He regarded controversy among Christians as both trivial and harmful to Christ's kingdom. Donne was above all a peerlessly eloquent preacher, whose sermons radiate a supernal glow to this day. The puritans demanded the exaltation of the preaching office, and Donne, though far from being a puritan himself, did much to set a high standard for Anglican preaching. (I wish it could be honestly reported here that the standard set by John Donne has been maintained with a rigorous consistency throughout the Anglican Communion from that day to this.)

An important development in England under James was the Arminian movement which stemmed out of the teachings of the Dutchman Jacobus Arminius (1560–1609). Arminianism was a humane protest and reaction against the inhuman logic of Calvinist theology, especially the Calvinist doctrines of election and reprobation. Arminius wrestled with the question of whether man is saved or damned solely by God's decree, and he concluded that God must give man some freedom to choose his destiny. The Arminians concluded that there is indeed a predestination but that it is based, not upon God's decree, but upon God's foreknowledge of whether or not a man will choose to accept salvation. Christ did not die for the elect only as the Calvinists contended, but for all men; however, only believers in him can receive the benefits of his sacrifice. The Arminians agreed with the Calvinists that man can do nothing good of himself, that all is of grace, so they were not Pelagians. They believed, however, that man is free to reject grace, and also that man can lose grace once having received it.

In England the High Church divines took up the Arminian position and made it their reply to the Calvinism of the puritans. William Laud (1573–1645) arose in their midst as a stalwart and aggressive champion of episcopacy, of catholic liturgy as adapted by Cranmer in the Prayer Book, and of Arminian theology against Calvinism.

Laud is commonly and rightly regarded as the founder-father of what later came to be known as Anglo-Catholicism. In debate with the Jesuit Fisher he granted that the Roman Church is a true part of Christ's holy catholic Church, but held that the Church of England is the purest part thereof. The puritans distrusted and detested him; the Roman Catholics saw him as one of their own at heart. He was not so in fact; but as the first eminent representative of a kind of Anglican churchmanship which is always suspected of crypto-papalism he appeared to many as no true Anglican. Laud was a man of deep devotion and intense conviction. Unfortunately, and disastrously for the Church, he was also a bigoted autocrat. His fierce prosecution of nonconformists served to identify the Church of England with Stuart absolutism in the minds of those many Englishmen who smelled a new thing in the air—freedom of conscience as a divine right of man. It is a major tragedy of Anglican history that Laud, with his high principles, lacked the winsome spirit of

Hooker and Andrewes. This tragedy would bear several fateful consequences, one of which is of special interest to Americans: Laud's suppression of puritan worship and activity created a crisis which moved some puritans to become "pilgrims" whose pilgrimage would bring them at last to a stern and rock-bound coast.

[1] The story of these men, who they were and how they worked, is delightfully told by Gustavus S. Paine in *The Learned Men*. Thomas Y. Crowell Co.

[2] *Ibid*, vii.

Chapter Sixteen

The Royal Martyr

"Thy head or my head!"
Oliver Cromwell, to
King Charles I

To this day many Anglicans revere "Blessed Charles the Martyr" as a saint. To many others this veneration of the last royal practitioner of the Divine Right of Kings seems strange or perverse. If he was in any sense a saint it was because of his strictly personal life and character as distinct from his political ideas. And he was a martyr for Anglicanism. If he had given in to the demands of his enemies that the Church be turned into a puritan sect he might well have kept his throne and his head. He died rather than to sell out the Church.

Charles's father James had said that kings "sit on God's thrones" here below, and Charles inherited this belief. Anybody today who ponders this claim may well wonder whence it came. How could a Christian ruler, a follower of him who took upon himself the form of a slave, see himself as "sitting upon God's throne" as a lord over men, accountable directly and solely to God? The exercise of some historical imagination is required. In England, after the break with Rome, there was a great void in the power-structure which had formerly been occupied by the pope. If the pope was no longer to rule, somebody had to take his place. The idea of a sovereign, self-ruling people lay still in the future; the ruler had to be a man—under God and over the people. The logical candidate for the vacancy was the "most Christian king." Moreover, this age was discovering the Bible. David the King is the hero-saint of the Old Testament; the Son of David is the King of kings of the New Testament. There seemed to be amply sufficient scriptural warrant for the Divine Right of Kings.

Charles believed it with all his heart and soul, and accepted it as his vocation. When he said "I owe the account of my actions to God alone" he meant it humbly, religiously. But already, when he came to the throne in 1625, his concept of his calling was anachronistic. A hunger for representative government was in the minds of his more progressive subjects. It is hard to judge how aware of this was the young king, if he had any awareness of it at all. He had been well insulated against the surging new ideas of the age. He saw no need for his subjects to have any voice in national policy, or to have any concern about it, since God had given this burden to their king. In his view there was no place for Parliament or for any such body representing the social will of the people. He decided therefore to dissolve Parliament in 1629, and for the next 11 years Parliament had no meeting.

All government during this period was by royal decree. The Earl of Strafford represented the crown in civil affairs, and Laud, who became Archbishop of Canterbury in 1633, ruled the Church.

The Church was the nation in its religious aspect, and Laud was resolved to have complete unity in it. Here was the *Respublica Christiana*, in its Elizabethan Settlement, being applied with a vengeance. Within this scheme there was neither need nor place for any other religious body than the national Church. Unity, as Laud conceived of it, was uniformity in all details of belief, worship, and life. The law of the land prescribed how all things religious were to be done, and Laud's job was to enforce this law. He was thoroughly conscientious and conscientiously thorough about it. There

was much disorder in the Church, and he blamed the puritan clergy for much of the prevailing messiness. He was right
on the point of fact. The puritans tended to associate all
decency and order in church with popery and therefore were
inclined to go to the opposite extreme. Laud ordered that
such things as cock-fighting in the churches be stopped;
clearly such desecrations were common. He demanded that
the bishops be obeyed by all, and that the rubrics of the
Prayer Book be conformed to punctiliously. Failure to do so
was a criminal offense.

Between Laud and the puritans there was mutual detesta-
tion. It was a bitter age, and neither he nor they did anything
to sweeten it. It was Laud, however, who held the upper
hand, and so he is history's villain. The punishments dealt
out to puritans convicted of scurrilous pamphleteering were
incredibly savage, including such things as cutting off ears
and tongues, slitting noses, branding, whipping, and the gallows. Such penalties were liberally inflicted. Laud evidently
could not see that he was not accomplishing his purpose of
religious unification and pacification by such methods but
was only creating a vengeful hatred of the Church of England as then constituted.

Throughout the eleven years of government by royal decree, Laud was able to rule the Church as he saw fit. But in
1640 the Long Parliament was convoked, and militant parliamentarians marked both Laud and Strafford for destruction. In that year he was imprisoned, and four years later
brought to trial on charges of trying to alter the true protestant religion into popery. He was judicially railroaded to
condemnation and death. In this court action and in others,
the puritans showed themselves astonishingly unprincipled
in the administration of justice.

Concerning the effect of Laudianism upon the subsequent
shape and destiny of Anglicanism it has to be said that one
result of it was the permanent alienation of the puritan
movement from the Church. England would become a land
of many sects and chapels outside the national Church

largely because Laud had made "prelacy" a stench in the nostrils of so many. He was a man strong in courage and devotion, but born a hundred years too late.

The fate of the Church now linked up with the fate of the king. Charles, too, should have lived in another age. The whole tide of world change was running against him. He was against Parliament as an expression of people's government, but the parliamentary movement could not be stopped. Both Parliament and people were taking a growing interest in foreign policy, which in times past had been the sport of kings only. The revolution in religion had done much to bring about this change. Throughout Europe, the new protestant powers were lining up against the catholic powers. The English people were identifying themselves with the former, believing that their national welfare and very survival were bound up with the protestant cause. Increasingly, England as a whole felt a sense of being called to lead the protestant coalition. But Charles was incapacitated for leading the nation in this enterprise by two great handicaps: his devotion to royal absolutism, which was an article of faith with him, and his Roman Catholic wife, Henrietta Maria. He himself refused to turn Roman Catholic, and their six children were raised as Anglicans. The queen did not interfere in matters of state, and used her influence only to alleviate the lot of English Romanists. But England grew increasingly protestant politically, and English zeal for international political protestantism strengthened the movement toward parliamentary and representative government at home.

The powerful weapon in the hands of the parliamentarians against Charles was his need for money. Only tax levies by Parliament could finance the government's foreign and domestic programs.

In February 1638, at Edinburgh, representatives of the Scottish presbyterian ministry and laity signed the National Covenant, an act which was the real beginning of the English civil war. Because Charles was king of both Scotland

and England he had tried to establish the Anglican Church in Scotland. The National Covenant expressed open defiance, proclaiming presbyterianism the "true religion" and the only religion of Scotland. The king tried to put down the Covenanters by force, and suffered a humiliating defeat. The Scots invaded and occupied northern England in the summer of 1640. Desperately needing money and military support, Charles summoned what came to be known as the Long Parliament. A member of this Parliament whose star was rising was Oliver Cromwell, a puritan of towering genius in politics and in war.

When Parliament assembled in November 1640 its majority consisted of educated and wealthy men, much more plutocratic than democratic. Yet they represented the cause of people's government against monarchical dictatorship.

The English civil war was a struggle in which religious, economic, political and social factors all worked in such a way that it is impossible to treat any of these, such as the religious, in isolation from the others. Thus, when the Commons voted to bar the clergy of the Church of England from all legislative and judicial functions it was not on religious grounds; the members assumed that the clergy would simply vote for whatever the king wanted. Episcopacy and the Book of Common Prayer: these were the religious sanctions of the political institution of royalty, in the minds of the parliamentarians, and so they had to go. Parliament said to the Church of England as then established what Cromwell said to the king: "Thy head or my head!"

The year 1641 was one of triumphant open warfare against the Church. In May, Cromwell proposed the total abolition of episcopacy. Commons passed the bill, Lords rejected it. In September Commons resolved that "scandalous pictures" of the Trinity, images of the Blessed Virgin, all crosses and "superstitious figures" should be removed from churches. (The puritans generally regarded any and all visual religious art as "superstitious.") The king's reply was to tell the House of Lords that he was prepared to die if need be in defense of the doctrine and order of the Church of England.

The impasse between king and parliament could not be resolved by peaceful means and the war followed. It was as a general in the field commanding the Roundheads (parliamentarians) against the Cavaliers (loyalists to the king) that Cromwell rose to supreme leadership. The war ended in the destruction of the monarchy and the establishment of that strange interlude in English history called the Commonwealth. Charles paid with his blood for having done what he was sure was his duty to God, and for the mistake of losing the war. He was legally murdered by his enemies, not lawfully executed. The court proceedings were a judicial farce. He faced his accusers, and at last his executioner, with a majesty befitting a "most Christian king." His epitaph was unforgettably phrased by Andrew Marvell:

> He nothing common did or mean
> Upon that memorable scene,
>   But with his keener eye
>   The axe's edge did try;
>
> Nor called the gods with vulgar spite,
> To vindicate his helpless right;
>   But bow'd his comely head
>   Down, as upon a bed.

The public execution took place on January 30, 1649. When the severed head was held up to view the soldiers cheered; but a loud cry of anguish and sudden revulsion went up from the crowd. Undoubtedly, if the king had triumphed in the war, his enemies would have been dealt with as traitors. In a world in which conflict seems a very law of existence, all history cries *Vae victis!* Nevertheless, the killing of Charles came to be regarded by most Englishmen as "a crime against England even more than against Charles," in G. M. Trevelyan's words.

With the overthrow of the monarchy the Church of

England was outlawed and the nation was made officially puritan under the "rule of the saints." This the people patiently endured for a dozen years; but once the virtuous dictator Cromwell was dead they got what they wanted—a return to monarchy. With the monarchy would return the Church of England, with its bishops and Prayer Book. But it would be a going forward, not a turning back.

Chapter Seventeen

The Caroline Divines

Love is that liquor sweet and most divine
Which my God feels as blood, and I as wine.
George Herbert, *The Agony*

The true life of the Church, against which the gates of hell cannot prevail, is a life largely hidden from the historian and known only to God. So it was in the age of religious revolution in England. Being preoccupied with figures like Henry VIII, Wolsey, the popes, Laud, and Cromwell, we easily forget that these eminent people were not the Church. At best and at most they were members of the Church in such positions of power that they affected the Church as a temporal institution in its passage through time. Throughout these tumultuous years, the true life of the Church was inconspicuously but invincibly carried on in the lives of the faithful.

The men known to history as the Caroline divines were not themselves little people known only to God; nevertheless to know them is to know the faith and feelings of the Church as such in their age. They are important for another reason. Churchmen of later times, representing diverse schools of theology and churchmanship, have been profoundly influenced by them. As a body, these men have been the most influential Anglican thinkers about God, the Church, salvation and the means of grace.

A few general observations about them may be offered.
The Anglicans regarded both Roman Catholics and puritans as being too exclusive in apprehending the truths of the
Gospel. In their "via medianism" they rejected both the
Roman and the puritan kinds of infallibilism. Hooker put
the position succinctly: "Two things there are which greatly
trouble these later times: one that the Church of Rome cannot, another that Geneva will not, err." The Anglicans would
not set up any infallibilism of their own. As one of their
divines, John Hales, put it: "Infallibility either in judge-
ment, or interpretation, or whatsoever, is annext neither to
the See of any Bishop, nor to the Councils, nor to the
Church, nor to any created power whatever." Hales is not
denying God's own infallibility or that a man may be guided
into all truth by the infallible God. What the Anglicans rejected was any infallibility resident in, or belonging to, pope,
or church council, or Bible, or any such "created power."
Man, they held, has no need of any infallible guide other than
God himself. God makes known to his people through Jesus
Christ what they need to know for their salvation. The
Church is the community of witness to this revelation, and
as such the Church is constantly taught and guided by the
Holy Spirit who leads it from age to age into all truth. The
Anglican view is not that the Church *cannot* err but that it
does not err in its teaching and providing the "things nec-
essary to salvation." God preserves it from error, but this
infallibility is God's, not man's.

The Anglicanism of the revolutionary age was marked
by a freedom and freshness in the interpretation of traditional truth. George Herbert's couplet, quoted as the text
for this chapter, illustrates this:

> Love is that liquor sweet and most divine
> Which my God feels as blood, and I as wine.

The sacramental theology expressed here is entirely orthodox and traditional, but there is a freedom in the Anglican

poet's statement of it that is no mere poetic license. It was a fresh new way of looking at old truths.

Little Giddings

Nicholas Ferrar (1592–1637) founded what the puritans scornfully called the "Arminian nunnery" at Little Giddings in Huntingdonshire. It was an effort to establish a quasi-monastic life on a family basis. Ferrar, a clergyman, and his family began the experiment in their manor house in 1626. Their life was ordered by a daily round of prayer within the monastic framework of the daily offices and the recitation of the Psalter. The communal routine was kept up from 1626 until the death of Nicholas in 1637. In 1646 the house was sacked by the puritans and the family scattered. Although Little Giddings remained unique as an experiment in family monasticism, it had a deep and lasting influence upon Anglican devotion.

George Herbert

All the world knows that Izaak Walton wrote immortally about the joys of fishing. Less known is the fact that he was a splendid biographer of such Anglican worthies as Donne, Hooker, and George Herbert (1593–1633). Herbert was a close friend of the Ferrars at Little Giddings, and a devout and diligent country parson as well as a poet. Walton tells how Herbert's rustic parishioners "would let their plough rest when Mr. Herbert's Saints'-bell rung to prayers, that they might also offer their devotions to God with him; and would then return to their plough. And his most holy life was such that it begot such reverence to God and to him, that they thought themselves the happier, when they carried Mr. Herbert's blessing back with them to their labor. Thus

powerful was his reason and example to persuade others to
a practical piety and devotion." One of Herbert's aphorisms
was, "Religion does not banish mirth, but only moderates
and sets rules to it." Here was Christian sanity in reply to
the fanatical condemnation of the pleasures of life which
was part of the puritans' hot gospel.

Herbert typifies a kind of Anglican clergy who have been
found in every generation: men of unusual learning or talent
serving in little country cures. There were many priests of
this type in Herbert's age, though few of course were his
equals in ability. The spiritual quality of the parish clergy
was higher than one might gather from reading history
books, and because the laity may be reasonably judged by
their clergy it is a sound inference that dispersed throughout the Church of England, in all ranks, was a good lot of
quiet, unostentatious "Prayer Book piety." A Church with
even a few parsons like George Herbert could hardly be the
synagogue of Satan which the puritans said it was.

John Cosin

Among the leading clergy who were deprived and exiled
during the Commonwealth was John Cosin (1594–1672),
Dean of Peterborough at the outbreak of the civil war. At the
Restoration he became Bishop of Durham and played an
important part in the re-establishment of the Church. During his exile, Cosin served as chaplain to Henrietta Maria's
household in Paris. Being forced to defend his perseverance
in Anglicanism against Roman Catholic adversaries Cosin
developed and strengthened the Anglican apologetical position. For a man of his age he had a remarkably ecumenical
mind. At the Savoy Conference in 1661 he was one of the
Anglican leaders who worked hard, but vainly, to achieve a
reconciliation between the Church and presbyterianism. But

it is as a liturgiologist that he is chiefly remembered. He contributed much to the revision of the Prayer Book in 1662.

Jeremy Taylor

Famous in literature as an essayist, Jeremy Taylor (1613–1667) is eminent in the Church as an Anglican moral theologian. His devotional writings, especially *Holy Living* and *Holy Dying*, are classics of well ordered yet fervent devotion, and beautiful prose. His *Liberty of Prophesying*, published in 1647, is an eloquent plea for a Christian forbearance born of charity in religious disputes. It has to be added that when he became Bishop of Dromore he treated nonconforming presbyterians with the harshness characteristic of his age. Moreover, in his *Dissuasive from Popery* (1664) Taylor seems to forget his own professed principle of generous respect for one's theological opponents.

Taylor regarded his compendium of moral theology, *Ductor Dubitantium, or the Rule of Conscience*, as his most important work. It is an erudite compilation of the moral doctrine and casuistry of both Roman Catholic and continental protestant moralists, to be used by the clergy in the confessional for the guidance of souls. Since Taylor's day the work has been widely neglected, but not forgotten, and with the modern revival of moral theology in Anglican concern it is being more generally studied and used as a basis for further development of moral theology.

Thomas Ken

A junior contemporary of Herbert and Cosin was Thomas Ken (1637–1711), Bishop of Bath and Wells. Though not a peer of Herbert as a poet, he wrote some splendid hymns which both express and inspire a "down-to-earth" devotion, such as:

> Direct, control, suggest, this day,
> All I design, or do, or say;
> That all my powers, with all their might,
> In thy sole glory may unite.

Ken's eucharistic devotion represents the Anglican combination of firm belief with reticence of statement, as seen in this passage from his *Exposition on the Church Catechism*:

O God Incarnate, how Thou canst give us Thy flesh to eat and Thy blood to drink, how Thy flesh is meat indeed and Thy blood is drink indeed, how he that eateth Thy flesh and drinketh Thy blood dwelleth in Thee, and Thou in him, how he shall live by Thee and shall be raised up by Thee to life eternal, how Thou who art in heaven art present on the altar, I can by no means explain; but I firmly believe it all, because Thou hast said it, and I firmly rely on Thy love and on Thine omnipotence to make good Thy Word, though the manner of doing it I cannot comprehend.

James Ussher

A biblical chronology known as Ussher's, which contains some very disputable dates, is often published with the Authorized Version. It is the work of James Ussher (1581–1656), a native of Ireland who became Primate of Ireland in 1625. Unfortunately, he is mostly remembered for his biblical chronology, which sets the date of creation at 4004 B.C.—in October. Let it never be said that he hedged on details. Ussher was in fact a very learned man, and very independent. He was no slave to consistency. Though a strong Calvinist in theology he was a staunch friend and admirer of Laud. His defense of praying for the departed was sufficiently catholic to be reprinted as one of the *Tracts of the Times* in the Oxford Movement of the 1830's. He was a fine patristic scholar, and he thoroughly ransacked such early authorities as Ignatius and Polycarp to find ammunition for defending episcopacy against presbyterianism.

John Pearson

"Pearson on the Creed" is a household word in Anglican divinity. It is the *Exposition of the Creed* by John Pearson (1612–1686), Bishop of Chester. The exposition of the Apostles' and Nicene Creeds is rooted in the Scriptures and the church fathers. It has one serious defect, which is rather generally shared by his learned contemporaries, and that is that his theological reasoning is historical at the expense of the contemporary. These men were bent upon proving their case against their opponents from the Bible and the early Church, so much so that their theology often lapses into antiquarianism. Anglican theology had to learn to listen to the voices of the science and philosophy of the dawning new world.

William Chillingworth

"The Bible, I say, the Bible only, is the religion of protestants," said William Chillingworth (1602–1644). This statement has been quoted ever since, and regrettably apart from its context in the treatise *The Religion of Protestants*, where it is followed by this explanation:

Whatsoever else they (the protestants, meaning the Anglicans) believe besides it, and the plain, irrefragable, indubitable consequences of it, well may they hold as a matter of opinion: but as a matter of Faith and Religion, neither can they with coherence to their own grounds believe it themselves, nor require belief of it for others, without most high and most schismatical presumption.

Chillingworth distinguishes the Anglican view of the authority of the Holy Scriptures from the Roman and Calvinist views. He holds that nothing may be taught as necessary dogma unless it can be scripturally attested as part of the original apostolic faith. An extra-scriptural opinion may be true, and important, but it may not be imposed as *de fidei*.

When Chillingworth was about 11 he was converted to Roman Catholicism and went to Douai to study. After two years there he returned to his home at Oxford, and finally returned to the Church of England. Like Ussher he was remarkably independent in his thinking. His ordination was delayed by his inability in good intellectual conscience to subscribe to the 39 Articles. When he eventually overcame these scruples it was by honest thought rather than expedient compromise.

The emerging pattern

In the works of the Caroline divines we can trace a definitely emerging pattern of Anglicanism. Despite the strict Laudian regulation of worship and popular preaching it is evident that the Church's theologians enjoyed a large intellectual freedom within the broad framework of the official doctrinal structure. Thinking freely and independently the Anglican divines reached a consensus about primary matters of faith. Nothing in this consensus was more important than the principle that tradition has a valid place in faith and worship (which the puritans denied) but that it must always be tested by the Scriptures and may not contradict the Scriptures. This principle has preserved Anglicanism from bibliolatry while keeping it biblical.

One more characteristic of the Caroline divinity which was to become permanently and centrally Anglican is this quality described by Paul Elmer More:

If the Anglican differs from the Romanist or the radical Protestant, it is because more definitely and consciously than either he justifies his belief by the pragmatic test of experience, namely: "Does it work?" It is not that he rejects authority for an unchecked individualism; he sees that his personal experience is no more than a fragment of the larger experience of mankind, and must be controlled at every step by the accumulation of wisdom which is the voice of the Church. What he rejects is the Absolute of authority based on *a priori* theories of infallibility. Rather, looking within and without, he asks the consequences of believing or not believing. How does acceptance of the dogma of the Incarnation work out in practice? Does faith bring with it any proof of its objective validity?[1]

More goes on to note the Anglican "pragmatism" in the doctrines of priesthood, episcopacy and the eucharist, and rightly concludes:

Not only in the seventeenth century but from the time of Henry VIII to the present day, if there is any outstanding note of the English temper it is a humility of awe before the divine mysteries of faith and a recognition of the incompetence of language to define the ultimate paradox of experience. . . . As Cudworth, one of the most metaphysical of the Caroline theologians, expressed it, "neither are we able to inclose in words and letters the life, soul, and essence of any spiritual truth, and as it were to incorporate it to them."[2]

[1] Essay in More and Cross, *Anglicanism*, xxxiii.
[2] *Ibid*, xxxvii.

Chapter Eighteen

Commonwealth and Restoration

New Presbyter is but Old Priest writ large.
John Milton, *On the new forcers of Conscience under the Long Parliament*

On May 19, 1649, the English republic was born. Parliament proclaimed:

England shall hereafter be governed as a Commonwealth, or Free State, by the supreme authority of this nation, the representatives of the people in Parliament, and by such as they shall appoint and constitute under them for the good of the people.

The "republic" was never a democracy, and soon became a dictatorship. After only 11 years of it England would return to monarchy. But the effects of this puritan revolution were profound and permanent. Modern Britain and the United States of America are what they are, politically and culturally, because of this brief upheaval of three centuries ago.

In the triumph of puritanism, Anglicanism was overthrown. The victors were determined to establish a state church which would be presbyterian in polity and Calvinist in doctrine, and they did so officially in 1646. Two years earlier, the Prayer Book had been declared illegal by Parliament and had been replaced by the *Directory of Public Worship*. In the Directory, careful instructions were given as to how public prayer, preaching, and other rites were to be performed; but no form was provided for anything—not even the Lord's Prayer.

The next step in the puritan revolution was to replace the Anglican ministry with a presbyterian one. In the new order, the congregations were ruled by ministers (only presbyters, no bishops or deacons). The ministers in turn were ruled over by the classes, or district synods; and over the classes were the provincial and national assemblies. As a system, this presbyterian order was well organized, tightly disciplined, and should have been successful in operation. But the presbyterians faced determined opposition from a rising body of puritans who came to be known as the independents. Presbyterianism had developed in Scotland as a rigid and strongly clerical polity, and it soon became clear to many Englishmen that there would be no more freedom of conscience or expression under the presbyters, the classes, and the assemblies than there had been under Laud. John Milton, who was among the independents, voiced this anxiety when he quipped that new presbyter was but old priest writ large.

Moreover, Cromwell was not a presbyterian but an independent. He believed in religious toleration. "I meddle not with any man's conscience," he said, and meant it. He did not tolerate Roman Catholics or Anglicans, but this was for political reasons: they were enemies of his state.

Not all Anglicans by any means were implacably opposed to the commonwealth. In fact, more than half of them accepted the new religious order and went on attending their parish churches, taking what was offered them in doctrine and worship. Moreover, Anglican church life as such did not cease to be, even though it was under the ban. John Evelyn reported that he knew of at least one church in the heart of London where the Prayer Book worship was openly conducted. The episcopate was in danger of extinction, but it survived the period, and ordinations to the priesthood were carried on in secret.

It was only the unreconstructable Laudians who chose

to be irreconcilable enemies of the puritan republic. But there were some of them, and though a small minority they were united by powerful convictions and loyalties. They remained sure throughout their troubles that the Church of England as they knew and believed in it had a future because it was God's Church in England, and they considered it their calling to keep the Anglican faith until the day of return. Because of their continuing conviction that monarchy and episcopacy were inseparable they kept in touch with Charles II, the king in exile, and used all their influence to keep him in the Anglican way lest he turn either to Roman Catholicism or to Presbyterianism.

The puritans unwittingly helped their enemies' cause by making religion a burden, bore, and vexation of spirit to the common man. Most pleasures were proscribed as snares of the Devil. The most innocent games and folk dances were sternly forbidden. A woman might be respected, if she proved beyond peradventure that she was a faithful wife or a good mother; otherwise, being a woman, she was suspect as a daughter of Eve. Music, except in hymns, was banned. In the churches all art was destroyed as idolatrous. The puritan moral code was imposed upon everybody by persuasion of whip, pillory, prison and gallows. Sundays were turned into a dreary ordeal in which one was hardly permitted to turn around. This inhuman rigorism led to the inevitable reaction against the puritan conception of godly living.

In justice and truth, however, it must be noted that English character, political institutions, and religion owe much to the puritans. Although puritanism narrowed the mind, it strengthened the conscience and will. It inculcated devotion to principle, at whatever cost to the individual. Thousands of puritan clergymen, when the commonwealth was ended and their foes were in power again, accepted poverty and deprivation rather than to compromise their principles. The puritans of the 17th century were not democratic in the modern sense of the term, but their religion and

ethic formed the matrix out of which Anglo-Saxon democracy would emerge. Calvinism engendered in its adherents
a spiritual independence enabling them to stand against the
powers of this world. This independency in face of the
established order and powers became a vital element in
English and American democracy. A direct product of it is
the axiom in our society that the individual man at bay
against "society" may be right and "society" wrong.

Yet the dominant tendency toward radical independency
and individualism in religion proved to be a weakness in the
commonwealth. Sects and schisms proliferated in such a
way as to make unity impossible. Puritanism could not
create a church to replace the Church of England.

Oliver Cromwell died in 1658 and his son Richard succeeded him as Lord Protector. Oliver's last years were made
wretched by personal sorrows and by the realization that
his subjects did not love him. Richard had no heart for the
kind of government in which Oliver believed, so he resigned
the protectorate in 1660. A new Parliament, elected especially for this purpose, invited Charles II to return from his
exile in Holland and to take the throne.

Charles II

In the Declaration of Breda, issued before his enthrone-
ment, the new king promised a general pardon to all but a
few who had been directly involved in killing his father, and
some measure of religious toleration. "We do declare a
liberty to tender consciences," he said, "and that no man
shall be disquieted or called in question for differences of
opinion in matters of religion which do not disturb the peace
of the kingdom." The presbyterians, who controlled Parliament at the time, and the independents took this to mean
full toleration and equal rights for their beliefs and practices.
They were mistaken. Episcopacy was soon fully restored.
The puritans hoped to prevent the restoration of the Prayer

Book and of such odious rites and ceremonies as wearing the
surplice, kneeling at holy communion, bowing at the name
of Jesus, and signing with the cross in baptism. Charles
agreed to a conference on such issues, which took place at
the Savoy Hospital in August 1661. The puritans presented
a long list of grievances, mostly liturgical. The Anglican
bishops at the conference were convinced that what the
puritans were aiming at was a total abolition of the Prayer
Book order of sacraments and worship, and they refused to
concede an inch.

It was generally agreed that the Prayer Book needed revision and updating. This task was done at the winter session
(1661–62) of the Convocation. Here again the puritans tried
to "purify" the liturgy and were totally repulsed. Many
minor changes were made. A form of baptism of adults was
provided; a commemoration of the dead was included in
the prayer for the Church; the words "sanctify this water to
the mystical washing away of sin" were added to the baptismal rite. An act of uniformity required that the revised
Prayer Book be put into use on St. Bartholomew's Day,
1662. All clergy and schoolmasters were required to declare
that they would use this 1662 Prayer Book and no other, and
also that they held it unlawful to take up arms against the
king. It was further provided by the act that all clergy who
had not been episcopally ordained should be deprived.

Thus the Church of England was restored, and the new
leaders of church and state worked together to create national unity on a religious basis. Their ideal was that of
Elizabeth: full comprehension of all Christians by the national Church. But it proved impossible. The Church of
England could not absorb and assimilate either radical
protestantism or Roman Catholicism. Once this became
evident, as it soon did, the powers in command devised a
new policy: that of making the nonconformist a second-class
citizen. A series of acts known collectively as the Clarendon
Code was passed by Parliament. Their sum and substance

was that a person must be a communicant of the Church of England in order to enjoy the full rights of citizenship. The Test Act in 1673 required any man holding civil or public office in the land to receive holy communion in the Church of England, to denounce transubstantiation, and to take the oaths of supremacy and allegiance. This act was aimed against both puritan and Roman Catholic subversive elements. Protestant nonconformity and Roman Catholicism together were placed outside the official religious pale, and for the same reason—political rather than religious. Because of the wide and deep wall between them they were never able to make common cause against the Church.

The Cambridge Platonists

In order to get a fully comprehensive view of the religious situation in England in the Restoration period, it is necessary—and refreshing—to turn from the political and sectarian turmoils to a group of Churchmen known as the Cambridge Platonists.

The earlier Anglican apologetics had been worked out on a traditional and authoritarian basis. It had been assumed that if a doctrine or rite could be "proved" from the Scriptures and the early Church fathers, no reasonable Christian would question it further. But some learned and devout Churchmen at Cambridge knew that a new approach and method was needed, one which would allow the proper use of the critical reason in arriving at religious conviction. These men, the "Cambridge Platonists," were not in fact philosophical disciples of Plato. They were closer to the ancient Neoplatonists who had combined Christian faith with that Platonic mysticism which holds that man is made for communion with eternal verities. They believed that God touches man directly in the mind; hence their golden text: "The spirit of man is the candle of the Lord" (Proverbs 20:

27). On this premise, they saw no reason why men truly living with God should not live peaceably with one another even while disagreeing in opinions.

In this school is the beginning of what is commonly called the Broad Church party in Anglicanism. These men were for the most part originally puritans who acquired the spirit of Hooker and became strong Churchmen. Though they exalted reason—one of them calling it "the very voice of God"—they were not rationalists setting reason in the place of God. They were devout souls who trusted in reason, not in itself but as "the candle of the Lord" which the Holy Spirit can set afire with divine truth.

The wisdom and devotion of this small group of learned men gave to the renascent Anglicanism of the Restoration a spiritual authority which was sorely needed. By its nature, the Cambridge "movement" could not become a nation-wide mass movement. It served only to draw and knit to the Church some people of superior intelligence, learning, and desire for both God and truth.

The "Glorious Revolution"

Charles II is better known for his mistresses than for piety or statesmanship, and understandably enough, for he had considerably more of the former. He was charming and amiable, without serious convictions or principles. In religion he tended to scepticism, but he had an emotional and esthetic bent toward Roman Catholicism. He evidently wanted to revive absolute monarchy and to restore Roman Catholicism, but he lacked the ability and character to do more than to dream about it. His brother James, Duke of York and next in succession, was a Roman Catholic. Early in 1669 Charles told James and several intimates that he wanted to turn Roman Catholic and eventually to restore England to Rome. This scheme fitted in with his desire for an alliance with catholic France against protestant Holland.

But Parliament was hard set against it, and in 1673 it passed the Test Act excluding any Roman Catholic—even a king— from holding public office in England. The protestant succession was henceforth a constitutional principle which has never been repealed.

In 1678 the nation was thrown into hysteria by the sensation of the "Popish Plot." A provocateur named Titus Oates had managed to convince many people that there was a Roman Catholic plot to assassinate the king, who would then be succeeded by James, who would restore the papal power over England. The panic lasted for three years, and many innocent people were accused and executed on charges of participation in the conspiracy.

Toward the end of his life, in February 1685, Charles embraced Roman Catholicism. James succeeded him. The new king, being a Roman Catholic, could not receive holy communion in the Church of England as the law required of all who held public office. Nobody believed his assurances that he fully intended to protect the Church of England as the established Church of his realm. "All the land quakes for fear!" wrote Abraham de la Pryme in 1687; "the jesuits and papists here bear all down before them, and many have been heard to say that they expect to wash their hands in hereticks' blood before next Christmas."

It happened that James had two daughters by his first wife, both of whom were protestant. One of these, Mary, had married the protestant William of Orange. Powerful figures in England approached William and Mary to invite them to come to England, by forceful invasion if necessary, to take the throne. Late in 1688 James saw that he faced sure defeat if he tried to keep his throne; so on December 18th he fled, dropping the Great Seal into the Thames. On the same day William entered London, and the "glorious revolution" had been accomplished without bloodshed.

Chapter Nineteen

The Age of Reason

Know then thyself, presume not God to scan;
The proper study of mankind is man.
Alexander Pope (1688–1744), *An Essay on Man*

One would probably have to be an Englishman of the 18th century to understand that age. As we approach it we should prepare ourselves for some odd and confusing things. The common impression today that the 18th century in England was a placid, uneventful, dull time, especially in religion, is remarkably off the mark.

The age formally begins with the accession of William and Mary in 1689. In religion, the Dutch William was an unenthusiastic Calvinist. His political goal was to curb France by means of an invincible coalition of protestant states. England was totally protestant in this political sense. But the Church of England baffled William. It was not at all protestant in the way and degree he should have liked to have it. At the outset of his reign he tried to make the Church comprehensive enough to take in the puritans, but the bill that would accomplish this failed to pass in Parliament. Among the proposed changes were the alteration of the term "priest" to "minister" in the Prayer Book, the elimination of some saints days, and making optional rather than mandatory the sign of the cross in baptism and the wearing of the surplice. When this effort failed the Tolera-

146

tion Act was passed, which was a concession that full national comprehension within the Church was impossible. This act exempted "their majesties' Protestant subjects dissenting from the Church of England from the penalties of certain laws." It granted freedom of public worship to protestant dissenters who affirmed the Holy Trinity, whose meeting houses were properly registered, and whose ministers subscribed to the doctrinal portions of the 39 Articles. All the civil disabilities of dissenters, however, were retained, so the toleration granted by this act in 1689 was very limited. Yet it was a step that would never be taken back.

The Nonjurors

For most Englishmen, the transition from the reign of Roman Catholic James II to that of Calvinist William and Anglican Mary was a "glorious revolution" without bloodshed, removing the threat of a Roman Catholic take-over. But some Anglican clergy could not in good conscience take the oath of allegiance to the new rulers. They had already sworn an oath to James, who was still living. On their reasoning he remained their only lawful king. Among these conscientious objectors were William Sancroft, Archbishop of Canterbury, Thomas Ken, Bishop of Bath and Wells, and Thomas White, Bishop of Peterborough. These men were Anglicans, not Romanists or dissenters, and this was a question of authority. To the Romanists, the pope was the supreme authority among men. To the dissenters and to most Anglicans, authority resided in the people as represented by Parliament. To these Nonjurors, authority under God was vested in the king.

The Nonjurors numbered some 400 clergy, with nine bishops, and among them were some of the Church's best men. They might have simply retired into lay communion, in which state they would not have been molested, but their conscience would not permit this. They held that the

Church of England could not be the true Church so long as it was under oath to the unlawful sovereigns. The true Church resided in them, the Nonjurors, and in the body of faithful laity who stood with them. The result was a schism. The Nonjurors kept in touch with the exiled King James, who, in 1694, nominated George Hickes and Thomas Wagstaffe to the episcopate. When these men were consecrated by nonjuring bishops, the Nonjurors had their own episcopate, and it would not die out until the last bishop in its line died in 1805. The schism of the Nonjurors was a grievous loss to the Church, for among them were men of preeminent learning, fervent devotion, and solid catholic convictions in an age of widespread heresy and dilution of Christian truth.

The attitude of the Nonjurors toward the oath of allegiance is the last serious expression in English history of the doctrine of divine right of kings. It rested on the premise that the king is a sacral being in himself, not merely a civil potentate, so that an oath of allegiance to him is absolutely binding for so long as he lives. This doctrine could not live for long in the new world that was being born.

The intellectual revolution

John Locke (1632–1704) is the philosopher whose views would provide the rationale of the American war of independence. In his *Essay concerning human understanding* he wrote:

It is plain to me that we have a more certain knowledge of the existence of a God, than of anything our senses have not immediately discovered to us. Nay, I presume to say, that we more certainly know that there is a God, than that there is anything else without us.

In Locke's view, the existence of God should be obvious to any normal mind, and most of his intelligent contemporaries shared this assumption. It was an age of tremendous intellectual expansion resulting from the use of such new inventions as the telescope, microscope, barometer and thermometer. The savants studied the world and almost unanimously reported that the Great Architect of the Universe had created a masterpiece. God was a superb designer and builder, as one could see by scanning the starry heavens above and the snowflake under the microscope as well as by scanning the ancient holy scriptures. The whole creation had become a bible.

But this bright new dawn brought with it a grave challenge to traditional Christian belief. Faith had hitherto rested upon revelation: that particular revelation of God to man of which the holy scriptures were the witness. It had been the role of Christian reason to interpret this revelation. Such thinkers as Augustine, Aquinas, Calvin and Hooker would have agreed about this as a matter of course. But in the theological revolution of the age of Locke the roles of reason and revelation were being reversed. In the new scheme, belief in God and knowledge of one's moral duties, in other words the believer's acceptance of the Christian revelation, would rest upon reason. The new style of believing came to be known as natural religion, as distinct from revealed religion. Its character is clearly sketched by Norman Sykes:

From this invasion of the province of theology by scientific concepts there followed also the vogue of Natural Religion. For the evidence thus adduced of the nature and purpose of God was open to men of all races, times, and places. Herein it contrasted favorably with the proofs of Revelation, which had been vouchsafed only to men of one generation, living at a particular time and place, and the records of which were wrapped up in sacred books, written in languages no longer understood by the people. Against the universality of this Natural Religion there came to be set the scandal of the particularity of Christianity. Moreover, from the contemplation of the starry heavens above, the champions of Natural Religion passed to that of the moral law, written, as they firmly believed, in the very heart of every man;

and likewise of universal range and validity. Indeed so far was
God from having left Himself without witness within the mind
of men, that He had implanted there the conviction of His
existence, of the duty of men to worship Him, and to imitate
His beneficence, and of a future state of rewards and punishments for mankind. Thus the traditional relationship between
Revelation and Natural Religion was reversed; and instead of
asking whether peoples who had not heard of Christ could be
saved, the question became whether Christianity added anything
necessary to salvation to the tenets of Natural Religion.[1]

Deism

The new mood in religion demanded a new theology, and
the result was the emergence of two antiorthodox systems
known as deism and Arianism.

The term deism must not be confused with theism, even
though deism is theistic and not atheistic. Deism is belief in
a supreme being who can be known by reason unaided by
revelation. It is theism completely rationalized. As one reads
the works of the deists of two centuries ago it is astonishing
to find how "modern" are the questions they raised—questions raised by religious liberals today as if they had never
been raised before. A man who knows the history of doctrine
aptly remarked, after listening to a sermon by Bishop James
A. Pike: "That man has one of the finest minds of the 18th
century!" Many of the questions raised by Bishop Pike and
other supposedly advanced theologians of today were in
fact old and tired questions by the time the deists got
through with them. They were questions such as: How
could Christ be divine if he had the limitations of a human
being? How can eternal pre-existence be reasonably attributed to Christ? How can rational minds be expected to
believe in the incomprehensible absurdity of the Trinity?

The deists were not an organized party. Their only bond
of union was their intent to emancipate men from super-

stitious bondage to the letter of the scriptures. The miraculous elements in traditional faith they condemned as incompatible with the ordered creation of an always reasonable and orderly deity.

The deistic assault upon the ramparts of faith called forth some vigorous orthodox apologetics for the new age. The most notable work of this kind was Joseph Butler's *Analogy of Religion*. Bishop Butler (1692–1752) saw in the deistic theology a vast oversimplification of faith. He argued that man can truly know God only as God reveals such knowledge to him, but in the Christian revelation an ultimately perfect reasonableness is to be found. Saving faith must not be identified with correct belief. Like any great theologian Butler was himself a man of prayer and child-like trust in God, and he maintained both by his pen and by his life that salvation is given to man through such filial faith and obedience.

Arianism

The term Arianism immediately suggests fourth-century Egypt, not eighteenth-century England. There was, however, a remarkable revival of Arius's heresy in the age of reason. The English Arians disliked the catholic creeds which the Church had retained. They were radical protestants who acknowledged the authority of the Bible only. They were strongly influenced by Socinianism, a movement named after an Italian protestant of two centuries earlier (Sozzini, or Socinus, 1525–1562). Socinus had taught that Christ was only a man, but a man so filled with divine wisdom that God had raised him to a position in which he is now a hearer of prayer. The Socinian christology dovetailed with the Arian concept of Christ as being less than God but more than man, and thus found its way into the mind of 18th-century English dissent. Its effect upon the worship and devotion of people whose ministers were infected by it was gravely subversive. It was found—and here is a salutary lesson for Christians of later times—that where worship is no longer offered to Christ it soon ceases to be offered to God.

By the time of George III's accession in 1761 the Arian revival had passed its peak, and the impulses which had gone into it went on to new forms of religious rationalism.

William Law

No survey of 18th-century religion can fail to give respectful notice to William Law (1686–1761), one of Anglicanism's finest spirits. Because as a Nonjuror he could not take the oath abjuring the Stuart claims to the throne, Law lost his Cambridge fellowship in 1715, but he remained in the Church's communion.

In a refutation of the arguments of the deist Matthew Tindal he demonstrated the limitations of reason as a means of attaining full knowledge of God; only faith, he held, can open man's eyes to the fullness of truth. Law effectively championed the cause of orthodox faith on a number of fronts, but it is as a practically helpful mystic and spiritual guide that he is best remembered. His *Serious Call to a Devout and Holy Life* has inspired innumerable readers to a more faithful discipleship. Among eminent Christians who have owned their profound indebtedness to it are Samuel Johnson, the Wesley brothers, and John Henry Newman. Law taught, and exemplified, a life of heavenly love working on a most down-to-earth level. One day a stranger came up to him, made sure of who he was, placed an envelope in his hands and disappeared. The envelope contained a bank note for a thousand pounds. Law used the money to establish a school for poor children. This is the kind of thing he meant by devotion, which he defined as "a life given, or devoted, to God."

Practical Christianity

Thomas Tenison (1636–1715) was one of the "Latitudinarians" of the generations succeeding the Cambridge Platonists. These men exalted reasonableness in belief and generosity in life to the throne which in more traditional religion was occupied by faith and zeal for holiness. Speaking of his generation in retrospect, Tenison said: "Practical Christianity was its talent and delight." This was not an empty boast. We have noted the very down-to-earth character of William Law's devotion. Many Churchmen who lacked Law's spiritual depth shared his awareness of their Christian duty to love and to help the poor. The new way of thinking about God as the infinitely benevolent general superintendent of the cosmos was theologically shallow, but it did seem to quicken in the hearts of believers a desire to imitate the divine benevolence in works of mercy.

Among the fruits of this religious humanitarianism was the charity school movement. The aim was to provide a rudimentary education for poor children so that they could read the Bible and other edifying literature. To provide such literature the Society for Promoting Christian Knowledge (still flourishing, and known as the SPCK) was founded in 1698. These charity schools grew to thousands in number. They were financed primarily by the voluntary contributions of middle-class Christians. This Christian philanthropy preceded by a century and a half the state's undertaking to provide rudimentary education for all the children of all the people.

Another outlet of "practical Christianity" was the hospital movement. Throughout the land, hospitals were built by private contributions inspired by the Church's preaching of the Christian duty of caring for the sick.

The Anglicans had no monopoly of this Christian humanitarianism. The dissenters were especially active in education, partly because their own children were excluded from most schools. The dissenting academies set a high scholastic standard and pioneered in new subjects and in teaching methods appropriate to the new age. In this matter, as in so many others, dissent has done the Church of England a valuable service by forcing it to be at its best in order to justify its privileged position.

[1] Norman Sykes, *The English Religious Tradition*, 54.

Chapter Twenty

Evangelicalism

In the evening I went very unwillingly to a society in Aldersgate street, where one was reading Luther's preface to the *Epistle to the Romans*. About a quarter before nine, while he was describing the change which God works in the heart through faith in Christ, I felt my heart strangely warmed. I felt I did trust in Christ, in Christ alone, for my salvation. And an assurance was given me that He had taken away my sins, even mine, and saved me from the law of sin and death.

John Wesley's *Journal* of May 24, 1738

Pascal remarked that if Cleopatra's nose had been shorter the whole face of the world would have been different. It could likewise be said that if John Wesley had not had his "Aldersgate experience" the whole spiritual face of the English-speaking world would have been different.

Throughout the "age of reason" there developed in the Church of England a progressive spiritual sclerosis. Churchmen came to despise "enthusiasm," by which they meant something like what we mean today by "extremism"— carrying a good thing too far beyond the limits of moderation. This attitude had become in fact a condemnation of spiritual passion and zeal for holiness.

The Wesleys

The story of the evangelical revival is by no means simply identical with the Wesley story, but apart from the Wesley brothers it is *Hamlet* without the Prince of Denmark.

John Wesley (1703–91) was the 15th of a family of 19 children born in the rectory of Epworth, where his father was rector. While at Oxford studying for holy orders he joined a group of devout young men who were trying, amidst the prevailing worldliness and rationalism, to live a disciplined spiritual life. They were strict Churchmen trying to obey every rubric to the last jot, and because they so sedulously cultivated method in their devotion they were dubbed "methodists" in derision. It was as a zealous young High Church priest that John, along with his younger brother Charles, offered his services as a chaplain in the colony of Georgia in 1735. While on the voyage they met a company of Moravian Brethren, a sect of German pietists who believed that a special "conversion experience" is necessary to salvation. The ship ran into a frightful storm and all the passengers were terrified except the Moravians. John Wesley felt that these people, who had had a conversion experience, were consequently possessed of a perfect peace and trust in God which he lacked. His ministry in Georgia was unhappy and unfruitful. For all his zeal he lacked tact, prudence, and compassion for weak and sinful souls. Early in 1738 he was back in England, frustrated and despondent. Then came his Aldersgate experience in which he was born again. From that event may be dated one of the most incredibly energetic, prolonged, and revolutionary ministries in all Christian history.

George Whitefield

In 1735, Bishop Butler said to the Reverend John Wesley: "I once thought you and Mr. Whitefield well-meaning men;

but I cannot think so now. Sir, the pretending to extraordinary revelations and gifts of the Holy Ghost is a horrid
thing, a very horrid thing." Here spoke one of the greatest
Anglicans of the 18th century to another one. The vast gulf
between their understandings of their religion was the gulf
which in the end would separate some evangelicals—not all
—from the Church. Those who followed Wesley would become Methodists outside the Church[1]; the followers of
Whitefield would remain Anglicans.

George Whitefield, eleven years John Wesley's junior,
joined the "methodists" at Oxford in 1735. Much of his
ministry was in America, where in 1740 what came to be
known as the Great Awakening in New England resulted
from his preaching. Unlike Wesley, Whitefield was not an
organizer. His supreme gift was preaching repentance.

There were irreconcilable differences of belief between
Wesley and Whitefield. In their concepts of grace, Wesley
was an Arminian and Whitefield a Calvinist. Wesley taught
a doctrine of perfection, according to which a Christian can
attain right ruling motives—love for God and for his neigh-
bor—and thus be freed from sin. This smacked of Pelagianism. It is not always recognized, by those who criticize the
Church for often excluding Wesley from the pulpit, that he
was suspected by thoroughly responsible people of dangerously false doctrine. Another reason why Wesley's following
developed more and more independently of the Church was
the fact that he could brook no authority except his own.
The Church of his time was far from authoritarian, but it
had some rules and order. Of Wesley's genius for organization, Leighton Pullan rightly says that it "made everything
in Methodism begin and end in his own authority. He
wielded that supremacy for the promotion of holiness with
untiring activity, with extreme self-denial, with tact, with
dignity, with the courage that would always look a mob in
the face. But these eminent gifts, used in the service of the
Master, must not blind us to the dangers of his teaching. If
in the latter part of his career he openly violated the con-

stitution of the Church, he threatened the doctrine of the Church far earlier. His triumphant sermon on Free Grace directed against the Calvinism taught by Whitefield probably did more than any other sermon to bring English Calvinism to the grave. But Whitefield, and not Wesley, was with the Church when Wesley taught the possibility of sinless perfection being attained by man in his present state of existence."[2]

Something must be said of Charles Wesley. He is best remembered as a hymn writer, having written some 6500 hymns in all, many of which are still sung in most Churches today. Charles lacked John's genius for leadership, but he was stronger in reasonableness, gentleness, patience and charity. He did his utmost to keep methodism within the Church.

One extraordinary woman played a major part in the evangelical movement: Selina, Countess of Huntingdon (1709–91). She saw that the movement had been largely confined to the poor, and resolved to bring it redemptively to bear upon her own class, the rich and high born. She built chapels throughout the land to serve as evangelical conventicles, and founded a college at Trevecca in Wales to train evangelical ministers. Her chapels came to be known as "Lady Huntingdon's Connexion" and over this "Connexion" she ruled grandly and unilaterally, hiring and firing ministers according to her own taste.

More than anyone else, Charles Simeon (1759–1836) may be credited with having "domesticated" the evangelical movement within the Church. His loyalty to the Church earned for him the reproach of his evangelical critics that he was "more of a Church-man than a Gospel-man." After spending some years in an itinerant ministry like that of the Wesleys he came to believe that the evangelical principles could best be taught and imparted through the channels of the regular parish ministry. He helped to found the Church Missionary Society, which was to prove very influential in welding evangelical doctrine with missionary impulse.

The Methodist schism

It is needless to examine in detail the breach between evangelicals which resulted in the Methodist schism. The Church of England failed to provide ordination for men to serve as Wesleyan missionaries in the American colonies, despite the pleas of Wesley and other evangelical leaders. They wanted a missionary bishop for America who could ordain men to be pastors of the rapidly growing congregations of Wesleyan Anglicans. The English bishops were indifferent or hostile to the methodist movement. Then came the American war of independence, after which the bishops felt that they had neither responsibility nor authority to provide a ministry for the new republic. In 1784 John Wesley, now past 80, decided that he must abandon traditional episcopal order in the interest of souls unshepherded. He appointed two men of his following, Thomas Coke and Francis Asbury, to be "superintendents," and two others to be "elders," to administer the sacraments to methodists in America. Charles Wesley begged him not to proceed with this action. In 1785 John Wesley took the step of ordaining some men to the ministry though he was not himself a bishop. He was not acting entirely upon expediency. For years he had been convinced that in the New Testament bishop and presbyter are the same order; so, being a presbyter himself, he was also a bishop with the right to ordain in this emergency which resulted from the refusal of the duly authorized bishops to ordain. He had long been patient. His reasoning and his action are understandable. It was, however, the beginning of the schism between Methodism and Anglicanism which has lasted to this day.

Anglican evangelicalism, as distinct from methodism, followed a line of its own. Theologically it was moderately Calvinistic. Strategically, the most important difference was that the Anglican evangelicals worked through the parishes while the Wesleyans were itinerant. Among the Wesleyans there was an increasing tendency to set up "Church" and "Gospel" as antitheses, which inevitably led to a downgrading of "Church" as a vital part of "Gospel." The evangelicals who stayed in the Church were staunch Churchmen in belief, loyalty, and worship.

Summary

Most English historians agree with Lecky that the evangelical revival saved England from an upheaval corresponding to the French revolution. The poor were delivered from despair by the Gospel of God's love as brought to them by the evangelical preachers. Moreover, the movement created a social conscience which initiated beneficial social reforms and inspired a vision of a good society which could be achieved by means other than bloody revolution.

Evangelicalism was never a tightly integrated and disciplined movement, so there were large differences in teaching and emphasis. For example, only some evangelicals believed in the necessity of a "conversion experience." Most of the instant-conversionists left the Church with the methodists.

The ideas which made up the solid core of evangelicalism were these:

1. *The necessity of total commitment to a personal following of Jesus Christ.* Evangelicalism was partly a reaction against ecclesiastical formalism of the sort which assures one that all he needs for salvation is to belong to the right church, profess the right creed, receive the right sacraments and obey the right commandments: in a word, salvation by conformity. The evangelical replied that the Lord looks upon the heart and will of man, and there is no salvation except in the inner man.

2. *The God who saves is not simply an idea, or the Absolute, or the Supreme Being of the deists, but he is the God*

*who cares—who so loves the world that he gives his only-
begotten Son.* Here again, the evangelical theology is born
in reaction and protest against the arid rationalism of the
deists.

3. *The Christian man must pursue not an easy respectability but holiness.* Not all evangelicals shared John Wesley's doctrinaire perfectionism, the belief that a man can
arrive at perfection in this life; but all shared the perfectionism of the ideal of Christ's holiness as their goal.

4. *The state of a man's soul is to be judged not by how
he feels but by how he lives.* This evangelical axiom may
surprise some who note the evangelical tendency to emotional revivalism and conversion experiences. The evangelicals allowed themselves a very free rein in expressing their
ecstasies of repentance, conversion and rejoicing in the Lord.
But their leaders and preachers were constantly admonish-
ing them that faith without works is dead, that the regener-
ate new life must consist of active obedience of Christ in
all things.

Through the evangelical awakening the spiritual life of
the whole nation was wonderfully quickened. The one great
defect of the movement was its blindness to the nature of
the Church as the body of Christ. The eminent Congregational divine of the 19th century, Dr. R. W. Dale, said of
this:

The Evangelical movement contributed to the extinction among
Congregationalists, and, I think, among Baptists and Presbyterians, of that solicitude for an ideal Church organization which
had so large a place in the original revolt of the Nonconformists.
. . . It demanded as the basis of fellowship a common religious
life and common religious beliefs, but was satisfied with fellowship of an accidental and precarious kind. It cared nothing for
the idea of the Church as the august Society of Saints. It was
the ally of Individualism.[3]

[1] This seems an appropriate place to explain to any reader unfamiliar
with English ecclesiastical terminology that in England "the
Church" normally means the Church of England; the noncon-

formist and Roman Catholic parish churches are chapels. The 18th-century Methodists did not regard themselves as the Church, and after their separation from the Church of England they would have insisted that their "society" as they chose to call it was not to be confused with the Church.

[2] Leighton Pullan, *Religion Since the Reformation*, 145.

[3] R. D. Dale, *The Old Evangelicalism and the New*, 16.

Chapter Twenty-One

The New World

America is the only nation in the world that is founded on a creed.

Gilbert Keith Chesterton

On May 14, 1607, the Reverend Robert Hunt, chaplain of the Jamestown colony in Virginia, celebrated the eucharist on American soil, and with this event the history of Anglicanism in America began. It was 13 years before the Mayflower landed at Plymouth.

In 1664 the Dutch fort of New Amsterdam was surrendered to the English and New York was born. Anglican worship was then inaugurated in the old fort chapel. Trinity Church on lower Manhattan was founded by Anglican colonists in 1697.

The Anglican Church was fully established as the official Church of the colony in Virginia, and partially established in New York, the Carolinas and Georgia. The Church in the colonies was placed under the jurisdiction of the Bishop of London and it was entirely controlled from England throughout the colonial era. Parliament did not see fit to send out bishops to the colonies. This refusal put the Church in the colonies at a serious disadvantage against the dissenting sects, for the dissenters could ordain their ministers on the spot while the Anglican candidates for holy orders had to go to England to be educated and ordained.

Undoubtedly if the colonial Church had had its own episcopate its history would have been very different. It is possible,
for example, that the Methodists would have remained
Anglicans.

The Bishop of London sent out to the colonies men
known as commissaries, to represent him and to keep him
informed of the progress and needs of the overseas Church.
One of these to whom the Church was especially indebted
was Thomas Bray, who was sent out to Maryland in 1699.
He studied the colonial Church thoroughly, returned to
England and reported his findings to the authorities of
church and state. As a result of his eloquent pleading of the
case for the colonial Church two immensely influential
societies were formed in England: the Society for Promoting Christian Knowledge (SPCK), which promoted
theological education and literature, and the Society for the
Propagation of the Gospel (SPG), which would devote itself to providing missionary clergy and proper support for
them. The SPG would send out more than 300 clergy to
America during the colonial period.

The dire need was for an American episcopate, however,
and this was not met. The colonial dissenters were bitterly
opposed to having a single bishop on these shores. The New
Englanders especially were growing more and more anti-
royalist, and in their mind bishop and king were inseparable.
Some idea of the rancor of New England dissenters toward
bishops may be gained from a reminiscence of Alexander
Viets Griswold, who became a bishop of the American
Church in 1811. He recalled:

One of my neighbors, who was born about 1745, told me that,
when a child, he was taught that if bishops should come to this
country they would take from the people a tenth of everything;
children not excepted; and, as he happened to be the tenth
child of his parents, it was then, he said, his ardent desire that
he might immediately die in case a bishop were permitted to set
his foot on our shores.

Such was the common attitude of colonial dissenters toward episcopacy. The fear of the bishop was fundamentally political; "bloody prelacy" was regarded as the ecclesiastical sanction and support of royal tyranny. In point of historical fact their fear was quite anachronistic. Americans of the 18th century tended to hate and fear tyrannies which had been dead for many years in England. Laudian prelacy was one such dead bogey; in the mother country it had been long dead. It must be acknowledged, however, that for reasons other than "Laudian" the English bishops of the 18th century failed to make episcopacy seem indispensable or strongly desirable. Most people of the age saw them as lords spiritual rather than as successors of the Apostles and chief pastors of the flock of Christ.

Separation

The war of independence was a trial by fire for the Anglican Church in America. All its clergy had been ordained in England and, as a requirement of ordination, had taken the oath of allegiance to the king. This made them suspect in the eyes of their neighbors. Many of the clergy and at least a large minority of the laity were in fact loyalists, and thousands emigrated to Canada rather than take up arms against the crown. At the same time, George Washington himself was a staunch Churchman, and 35 of the 56 signers of the Declaration of Independence were Anglicans. A majority of Churchmen in the colonies supported the rebellion.

Once American independence was established there was widespread demand for the total abolition of Anglicanism from this land, as an inimical and subversive element. The Church was poorly prepared to meet this assault. In such colonies as Virginia and the Carolinas, where the Church had been legally established, there was now no longer any state support for the Church. In the northern colonies the

Anglican clergy had been mostly missionaries supported by English missionary society funds. The war swept away this support. There were no bishops in America to ordain, to confirm, to maintain discipline and order. In Virginia and Maryland the Church had received large and profitable grants of land from the crown, known as glebe lands. These were now confiscated by the state and the Church lost their revenue. The SPG had generously supplied the colonies with clergy. After the war, the Society announced that according to its charter it could provide missionaries only for British dominions.

The prospect on all fronts was bleak, but God did not leave the Church totally bereft of men of faith, ability and vision. One of these was Samuel Seabury of Connecticut (1729–96). Another was William White of Philadelphia. These two men were the founding fathers of the American Episcopal Church.

Reconstruction

After going to England for ordination White became rector of Christ Church, Philadelphia. He had set forth in a pamphlet his conviction that an American episcopate was impossible and that therefore the American Church should adopt a presbyterian ministry. The Churchmen in Connecticut were of no such mind, and determined to secure an American episcopate. In 1783 they chose Seabury to be their bishop, if he could secure ordination abroad. They instructed him to apply for consecration to the English primates, but if they could not or would not grant it to go to Scotland to seek consecration at the hands of the non-juring bishops of the Episcopal Church of Scotland. He found that in England there was a constitutional impediment, subsequently removed: a requirement that he swear allegiance to the British crown. He was consecrated by Scottish bishops on November 14, 1784.

Meanwhile, back in America William White had convoked an informal conference of Churchmen to plan strategy. They decided upon a general convention to be held in September 1785, with White presiding, in Philadelphia. This first general convention of the American Church was hardly auspicious in character. No delegates attended from New England, North Carolina, or Georgia. The Connecticut Churchmen would not attend a convention which was not presided over by a bishop. But this pioneer convention took several positive steps. It appointed a committee to prepare a constitution for the union of the Church on a national basis, and another committee to prepare a suitable revision of the Book of Common Prayer. It prepared and presented a memorial to the English archbishops and bishops requesting them to consecrate men chosen to be bishops in America. The memorial resulted in Parliament's removing the requirement of the oath of allegiance as a condition of consecration. The 1785 convention decided that the Church would be governed by a bi-cameral general convention consisting of two orders, clergy and laity, and meeting every three years. This triennial general convention would have power to legislate for the whole Church.

The Prayer Book committee hastily worked up a proposed book and submitted it to the English archbishops and bishops, who found it gravely defective. This proposed book expressed the preponderantly Low Church, ultra-protestant churchmanship of the delegates to the 1785 convention. Both the Nicene and Athanasian Creeds were omitted from it; the statement "He descended into hell" was omitted from the Apostles' Creed; the sign of the cross in baptism was made optional; the formula for absolution was entitled "A Declaration concerning the Forgiveness of Sins." In rejecting this proposed book the English Church leaders courteously but frankly made it clear that if the American Church was to be in communion with the Church of England it must compose a Prayer Book conforming to the standards of the mother Church. Eventually none of the proposed omissions was made except that of the Athanasian Creed.[2]

A second general convention met in Wilmington, Delaware, in October 1786. By this time three states had elected men to be their bishops: William White of Pennsylvania, Samuel Provoost of New York, and David Griffiths of Virginia. Griffiths was never consecrated because the Church in Virginia could not afford to send him to England. Provoost and White were consecrated at Lambeth Palace in February 1787. This made three American bishops, and three years later a fourth was added, James Madison of Virginia. In 1792 these four bishops jointly consecrated the first man made a bishop in America: Thomas Claggett of Maryland.

But a bitter controversy surrounded Samuel Seabury. Some doubted the validity of his consecration, hence the validity of his ordinations. The case against his legitimacy as a bishop was born of prejudices. He had been a loyalist throughout the war and had served as a chaplain to British forces. He was a definite High Churchman, and he had been elected by the clergy alone in Connecticut. He stood against all proposals either to curtail the powers of the episcopate or to provide a place for the laity in church government. The anti-Seabury movement failed to remove him from his office, but some of the issues involved in it would burst out later in new forms.

The American Prayer Book

It was clear that the hastily prepared proposed book of 1785 would have to be replaced at the convention to be held in 1789. Seabury had promised his consecrators in Scotland that he would try to persuade the American Church to model its Prayer Book upon the Scottish liturgy rather than the English one. This promise he kept, successfully, at the 1789 convention. The Scottish Prayer Book conformed more closely to Cranmer's 1549 Prayer Book than did the then official English Prayer Book of 1662. Consequently the American order for holy communion, which closely follows its Scottish pattern, expresses more clearly the traditional catholic understanding of the eucharist.

Permanent organization

At the 1789 convention the Church organized itself on a permanent basis. The young republic was actually a loose confederation of former British colonies now called states of the union, and it was now taking shape—in painfully disputatious travail—as a voluntary federation combining local freedom with a central government strong enough to preserve and to protect the union. The new Episcopal Church was organizing itself along parallel lines. To this day there are basic similarities of structure, distribution of powers, and inner checks and balances between the American republic and the Episcopal Church. One of these common features is the bi-cameral legislative body: the Congress of the United States and the General Convention of the Church. In 1789 the two houses were constituted as the house of bishops and the house of deputies. The latter consists of both clerical and lay deputies elected to membership of General Convention by their dioceses.

A reconciling and unifying spirit prevailed at the 1789 convention. The delegates unanimously resolved that Seabury's consecration was valid, and this action brought Connecticut, Massachusetts and New Hampshire into the fold. Seabury and his followers were not satisfied with all the actions taken, such as the refusal to restore the Athanasian Creed to the Prayer Book; but the more traditional Anglicanism which they represented won out on most issues. The house of bishops was established as a separate house and was given power to initiate legislation as well as to revise it. The Nicene Creed was restored, as were the sign of the cross in baptism and the descent-into-hell article in the Creed.

The Church's title

Whether the Episcopal Church should be classified as protestant or catholic remains a subject of apparently unending debate. The Church's choice of the title "Protestant Episcopal" has grown increasingly controversial through the years. The original choice must be understood in terms of the semantics and realities of the 18th century. To have called the Church simply Episcopal seemed insufficient because the Roman Catholic Church, which was especially strong in Maryland, was episcopal also. Why not "Anglican"? This strikes the 20th-century Churchman as the obvious and inevitable right word. But the term was almost unknown in the 18th century, and even if it had occurred to the first American Churchmen they would probably have rejected it forthwith as too English for the American Church. The word "protestant" did not at that time carry the connotations of anti-catholicism which it later required. It had come to mean any form of western Christianity not under the papal obedience, a sense in which the Episcopal Church clearly was and is protestant. The title "The Reformed Episcopal Church" was proposed, and rejected. "Reformed" has come to mean Calvinistic. The title "The Protestant Episcopal Church in the United States of America" was chosen at the 1789 convention with no noteworthy debate.[3] Probably most delegates regarded "in" as the most important word in the title, proclaiming as it does that the Church is *in* but not *of* the United States of America. Thus the Church *of* England became the Church *in* America.

[1] Quoted in H.G.G. Herklots, *The Church of England and the American Episcopal Church*, 79.

[2] The confession of faith known as the Athanasian Creed is in fact neither "Athanasian" in authorship nor "Creed" in a formal sense. It has never held equal authority with the Nicene and Apostles' Creeds, and where it has been retained, as in the Church of England, it is

primarily as a symbol of the Church's intention to remain orthodox.
[3] The General Convention of 1967 authorized the substitution of
"The Episcopal Church" for "The Protestant Episcopal Church" as
officially and legally permissible, with the result that both of these
alternative titles are equally correct.

Chapter Twenty-Two

Reform

The Church as it now stands no human power can save.
Thomas Arnold, Headmaster of Rugby, in 1832.

The evangelical movement had created in England a social conscience which could not rest in the presence of the wrongs and miseries suffered by slaves, the children of the poor, and all who were desolate and oppressed. Evangelical Churchmen contended that the Church must be the Christian conscience of the realm and they strove with no inconsiderable success to make it so.

Naturally, the world, the flesh, and the devil resisted. The evangelicals were commonly despised and ridiculed by more worldly Churchmen and evangelical clergymen were often subjected to discrimination. One bishop, Herbert Marsh of Peterborough, barred all evangelical ministers from cures within his diocese, thus provoking this expostulation from the pen of Sydney Smith:

How any man of Purple, Palaces, and Preferment can let himself loose against this poor working man of God [a poor evangelical curate] we are at a loss to conceive—a learned man in a hovel, with sermons and saucepans, lexicons and bacon, Hebrew books and ragged children—yet he is not good enough for Bishop Marsh, but is pushed out in the street with his wife and children, and his little furniture, to surrender his honor, his faith, his conscience and his learning—or starve![1]

One of the feminine lights of the evangelical movement was Hannah More (1745–1833), a lady of considerable literary skill. The books and innumerable tracts that poured from her pen found a universal readership among high and low, rich and poor. Dr. Porteous, Bishop of London, said of her tracts: "Here you have Bishop Butler's *Analogy*, all for a halfpenny!" Hannah More and her friends distributed Bibles and set up free schools for the poor. They may rightly be called the founders of free popular education in England.

There were numerous special-interest groups and societies within evangelicalism, the most famous of which was known as the Clapham Sect. Its members were mostly laymen who were distinguished in various fields and who were united by their strong conviction that true religion must express itself in energetic philanthropy. The best known member of this group was William Wilberforce (1759–1833), who devoted his long parliamentary career to the emancipation of all slaves within the British dominions. He saw the triumph of his labors on a great day in 1833, after nearly fifty years of unremitting striving for this single goal.

Church reform

It would be possible to mention many other godly Churchmen of the early 19th century who would adorn any age. None the less, this age was fraught with dark omens for English Christianity. In 1815, the year of Britain's glorious victory at Waterloo, less than a dozen people made their Christmas communion in Westminster Abbey. There was little vehement anticlericalism or dogmatic atheism in England. What Walter Lippmann in our time has called "the acids of modernity" had appeared and were dissolving the traditional faith of the people. There were several causes. The intellectual revolution of the 18th century had engendered a rationalism which regarded all supernaturalistic religion as superstitious. One of the heady ideas of the

French Revolution was that the Church is by its very nature an ally of the rich and powerful and therefore an enemy of the people. This idea found wide currency in unrevolutionary England. The industrial revolution had produced a vast and profound upheaval, out of which had come a class of crassly mammonistic merchants and industrialists more interested in investments than in their souls, to say nothing of the souls of others. A new working class, the industrial proletariat, had emerged also. The Church failed to move in and to establish itself in the urban slum areas which proliferated over the land, and so this new proletariat grew up largely outside the Church.

The Christian faith would have suffered more serious eclipse than it did but for the influence of two men who were not theologians or clerics but poets: William Wordsworth (1770–1850) and Samuel Taylor Coleridge (1772–1834). Wordsworth infused mystical feeling into the religion of his day. Coleridge's influence was more directly Christian. He anticipated and helped prepare the way for the Oxford Movement, or catholic revival, in his teaching that the Church is called to be no mere department of state but a divinely ordained spiritual body.

The Church was beyond saving, by any human power at any rate, said Arnold of Rugby in 1832. A growing number of thoughtful men shared his pessimism. Earlier in the century the prospect had not been so dark; there had been little positive hostility to God and the Church. But indifference and open hostility to the Church grew with the years. In the 1830s bishops were being burned in effigy. Many souls who were impatient for a better society saw the Church as a citadel of privilege and vested interests. The Church had in fact enjoyed a religious monopoly in the land ever since the Clarendon Code had been enacted in the time of the Restoration. Now there were growing demands upon Parliament for a legislative undoing of what had been done by the Clarendon Code. In 1828 the acts which had imposed civil disabilities upon nonconformists were repealed. The following year the Catholic Emancipation Bill did the same thing for Roman Catholics and made them eligible for Parliament. These steps did not mean the abandonment of the formal principle of the *Respublica Christiana*, as worked out by Hooker and established by Elizabeth, in which church and state are really one. On that principle, strictly applied, a man choosing not to belong to the state church renounces the spiritual basis of his citizenship and he has no ground for complaint if the state denies to him the rights of full membership of the community. In principle this concept was retained, but only as a concept. It was now established that in practice a man could be a non-Anglican without suffering any loss or curtailment of his rights as a citizen.

There were Churchmen at this stage who took the view that through all these vicissitudes of the Church as a legal and institutional establishment God was calling the Church of England to be more truly in nature and in practice the Church of the people of England. Thomas Arnold, whom we have earlier quoted, was a strong and high minded representative of this school. "When I think of the Church, I could sit down and pine and die!" he exclaimed in one of his darker moments. But he was not a man to sit down and pine and die. He saw in his superbly ordered school of Rugby a pattern of what the national Church could and should be; that is, a community of individuals, each moved by a noble spirit to give his best and his all for the good of the whole. In his *Principles of Church Reform*, published in 1833, he set forth a program for a truly national Church which would embrace all Christians of good-will—except Roman Catholics, Quakers and Unitarians. But so comprehensive a Church would have to be very vague and imprecise in dogma. Such an ordering of doctrine would be acceptable to Arnold and other men of his Broad-Church persuasion, but they were a minority, and the plan died for want of strong general support.

The Church needed some radical reforms within itself but seemed either blind to its own defects or helpless to do anything about them. Some of the most glaring of these defects were in its financial structure. The Church's wealth was distributed with monstrous inequity. Around the year 1830 some bishops were drawing annual incomes of up to 50,000 pounds, while half of the parish clergy received less than 60 pounds per year. The richest livings were owned by a few wealthy families who bestowed them upon their own clerical sons or friends. A clergyman's career was largely determined by his birth.

The bishops were commonly fine gentlemen and dignified grandees of the British Establishment. Those who belonged to their privileged class found little fault in them, but the masses of people did. The passage of the Reform Bill in 1832 gave the new working class a much larger share in the national government. Most of the members of this class were dissenters who saw the Church as a tool of the tory foe.

Radical reformers poured merciless abuse upon the Church. If all the facts of actual church life are taken into account, a fairly strong case for the defense can be made. There was little viciousness of life among the bishops and clergy. The pictures of parish clergymen drawn by such writers as Jane Austen and Oliver Goldsmith are by no means ugly, and are generally attractive. The Anglican parson of the late 18th and early 19th century was normally a Christian gentleman. One thing, however, he characteristically lacked, and that was a high sense of his mission as an ambassador and representative of Christ, and a proper reverence for his own office of priesthood. The Anglican clergy were all too generally obedient servants of the people who actually ran the country and ruled the land—the wealthy and the privileged. The fact that practically none of the impulse toward social reforms came from the bishops and clergy of the Church is itself sufficient evidence that these men generally failed to see their calling as Christian leaders to lead the holy war against evil and wrong.

"National Apostasy"

The year 1833 witnessed an event of revolutionary import
for the Church. This event began with a political reform
and ended with a sermon. The Church of England was
legally established in Ireland, where most of the people were
Roman Catholics. They had been required to pay tithes and
church-rates to the Anglican Church against their conscience and to the impoverishment of their own Church.
Lord Althorp introduced a bill in Commons early in 1833
which would reduce the Anglican bishoprics in Ireland from
22 to 12, the object being to ease the heavy financial burden
of the Irish rate-payers. In the eyes of some Churchmen this
was an interference by Parliament with the rights of the
Church.

Among the Churchmen outraged by this "interference"
was John Keble (1792–1866). On July 14, 1833, he preached
an assize sermon at Oxford on the subject "National
Apostasy"—his term for the Church's acquiescence in the
act of Parliament which would eliminate ten bishoprics in
Ireland. Keble's thesis was that the Church must be entirely
autonomous and free of state control. The immediate reaction to his sermon was the birth of what is variously called
the Oxford Movement, the Tractarian Movement, and the
Catholic Revival. A quiet and peaceable preacher had
stirred up a storm.

[1] S. Smith, *Works*, ii.

Chapter Twenty-Three

The Catholic Revival

In the last fifty years of the eighteenth century the Church had faded; in the first fifty years of the nineteenth it returned everywhere with astonishing vitality; and it returned not as morals or as humanitarianism, but as doctrine.

Charles Williams[1]

John Keble was no firebrand by nature or intent. But few sermons ever preached have created any such furor as did his Assize Sermon. As an immediate result of it about 7000 clergymen and almost 230,000 heads of families sent petitions to the Archbishop of Canterbury affirming their loyalty to the Church of England and her polity and doctrine. What had Keble said in his sermon to provoke all this? He had denounced the Irish Church Bill which would reduce the number of Anglican bishoprics in Ireland! It would be hard for any Christian of today to find moral fault in this eminently fair and just bill. But it was the principle underlying Keble's protest that exploded into life. That was the principle that the Church of England, as the true Church of the realm, was not properly subject to rule by the civil power and the secular politicians in any matter. In passing the Irish Church Bill laymen in Parliament were presuming to do what was for only the bishops to do, as God's appointed rulers of the Church.

Is the Church of England a mere creature and tool of the state, "the Tory party at prayer" as one unfriendly wag put it, or is it the creature and tool of Christ, ruled by Christ through his chief ministers on earth—the bishops of the Apostolic Succession? Keble's sermon put this question squarely before the whole nation. It was at Oxford in particular that the movement known as the Catholic Revival began.

The original leaders were a remarkable medley. Keble himself (1792–1866) was a child of the rectory, whose father had raised him on staunchly orthodox principles stemming from the Caroline divines. Throughout the 18th century and the early years of the 19th there had been quietly maintained, in countless homes like Keble's, a catholic faith and sacramental piety flowing like a strong, steady underground stream. After a few years at Oxford Keble resigned his fellowship and went home to help his father in his country parish. There he composed the poems which were published in 1827 under the title *The Christian Year*. In 1831 he returned to Oxford as a professor of poetry. He was now drawn to a circle of men who were alarmed by the menace to the Church of the liberal and reforming movements. Keble was profoundly at one with them. In his Assize Sermon he had spoken bitterly of "the fashionable liberality of this generation" which he saw as the apostasy of a Christian nation from its God. He spent the last 30 years of his life as a humble and holy parish priest, although contributing much literature to the movement. In his own way this first of the Tractarians was a prophet, poet, and saint.

John Henry Newman (1801–1890), by far the most widely known of the Tractarians, had been brought up under the strictest evangelical tutelage. The story of his life and career is so familiar from his famous autobiography, *Apologia Pro Vita Sua*, that we need not summarize it here. He dominated the movement for twelve years before joining the Church of Rome in 1845. Newman's supreme gifts were those of preaching and writing. For all the love and reverent regard given to him in both his Anglican and Roman careers, he was a strangely remote soul.

Newman's close friend and colleague in the early stage of the movement, Richard Hurrell Froude (1803–36), was a gay, witty romantic who loved to shock protestant Church-men with his clever strictures upon their Reformation heroes. The publication of some of his writings after his death had the effect of convincing many that the Tractarians were in fact cryptopapists out to undo the Reformation. In the end he did the cause no good.

Totally unlike Froude was Edward Bouverie Pusey (1800–82), Regius Professor of Hebrew and the supreme scholar of the movement. He was an austere man, but none the less a strong and effective leader. After Newman's defection he became the leader of the movement and remained so for half a century until his death. Among the major results of the Catholic Revival which were primarily the work of Pusey were the establishment of the eucharistic real presence of Christ as a cardinal conviction, the re-establishment of monastic life in the Church of England, and the widespread revival of auricular confession. On all counts, Pusey was the most influential man in the movement.

The tracts

The *Tracts for the Times* were an effort to follow up Keble's Assize Sermon with a nation-wide crusade for sound church principles "against Popery and Dissent." And they soon had the nation in an uproar. Reading them today we find this hard to understand, for the tracts are written in a pedantic and dully scholastic tone. But what the Tractarians were saying touched the besetting fears and prejudices of the multitude.

The tracts were published anonymously, though for some reason Pusey's were initialled. He and Newman were the chief authors. Some were simply reprints of writings by

Caroline divines whose doctrines the Tractarians claimed
to be reviving.

The first tract, written by Newman, appeared in September of 1833. It asserted the Apostolic Succession and
appealed thus to the Anglican clergy:

Christ has not left His Church without claims of its own upon
the attention of men. Surely not. Hard Master He cannot be,
to bid us oppose the world, yet give us no credentials for so
doing. There are some who rest their divine mission on their
own unsupported assertion; others who rest it upon their popularity; others on their success; and others who rest it on their
temporal distinctions. This last case has, perhaps, been too much
our own; I fear we have neglected the real ground on which our
authority is built—OUR APOSTOLICAL DESCENT.

Twenty tracts appeared before the end of that year. In
one of them Newman declared: "Popery must be destroyed,
it cannot be reformed." The protestant foes of the movement accused the Tractarians of Romanizing, but it is hard
to find anything in the text of the tracts in support of this.
Newman and his friends were sincerely and emphatically
anti-papal.

As controversy boiled throughout the Church, differences
and tensions developed among the Tractarians. The post-
humous publication of Froude's *Remains* in 1836 had a
mischievous effect. In them Froude had expressed a total
repudiation of the Reformation and an ardent devotion to
the medieval concepts of the Church and the Faith. Churchmen reading these shocking views suspected the Anglican
integrity of Froude's colleagues.

There emerged in the movement a concept of the Church
which came to be known as the branch theory, according to
which the English Church, the Roman Church, and the
Eastern Orthodox Churches are all branches of the one
catholic Church. In this view the English Church was seen
as the ecclesiastical *via media* between Rome and protestantism. Newman could not rest satisfied with it. He felt

impelled to pursue the line of thinking which Froude had begun. We do not know how Froude might have developed his position had he lived longer, but it was his premise that the medieval unreformed Church was the one true Church whatever its imperfections in human practice and institutional reality. Froude started from this premise, and Newman's mind moved toward it. The premise, as a conclusion, put the Church of England as a body separated from Rome in a hopelessly invalid position. But this was the Froude-Newman line, as distinct from the views of other Tractarians. Pusey held to the branch theory. Others, following Keble, were Anglican conservatives who wanted to restore the doctrinal standards and devotional practices of the Caroline divines, maintaining that the true catholicism of their Church was best found and fulfilled in that way.

Tract 90 appeared in February 1841. Never has so innocuously entitled a writing (with the possible exception of *Uncle Tom's Cabin*) had so shattering an impact. It was entitled "Remarks on Certain Passages in the Thirty-Nine Articles." Anyone reading the Articles of Religion for the first time, or the 50th, notes that their language is commonly vague, ambiguous, and capable of more than one interpretation. But in Victorian England the Articles were regarded by almost all as both a magisterial statement and a safeguard of the protestantism of the Church of England. Every ordinand, indeed every student at Oxford and Cambridge, had to subscribe to them. It was generally felt that such subscription by the clergy committed the Church to a securely protestant stance. Now came John Henry Newman in public print to analyze some of the Articles and to raise the question openly as to whether they might not be capable of a catholic interpretation. At this stage of his development Newman was insisting that there is a distinction between what is truly catholic and what is merely Roman and papal. He undertook to demonstrate this distinction in Tract 90. He took for this purpose 14 of the most anti-Roman Articles, among these being Article 22 which declares:

The Romish Doctrine concerning Purgatory, Pardons, Worshipping and Adoration, as well of Images as of Relics, and also Invocation of Saints, is a fond thing, vainly invented, and grounded upon no warranty of Scripture, but rather repugnant to the Word of God.

This Article, Newman argued, is not aimed against any truly catholic doctrine but only the "Romish" doctrine touching these matters. The "Romish doctrine" of purgatory, for example, is that doctrine which had become tied up with indulgences in the late medieval period. It must be distinguished from the properly catholic belief in paradise or the intermediate state.

The author of Tract 90 was denounced from pulpits throughout the land as a treacherous, deceitful scoundrel. Newman, a sensitive soul who found no joy in battle, retired more and more from public life and active controversy. In September 1843 he resigned his benefice of St. Mary's, Oxford. After two years of seclusion he entered the Roman Catholic Church.

In view of Newman's large and loyal following it is remarkable how few Anglicans followed him in his exodus to Rome. For this fact much credit is undoubtedly due to Dr. Pusey's leadership. Newman, unlike Pusey, had never been firmly and entirely sure of the Tractarian position. He had entered the movement at first while in a state of rebellion against the Calvinistic evangelicalism of his upbringing. He evidently craved the kind of ordered hierarchical authority which the Church of Rome could satisfy and the Church of England could not. Pusey, by contrast, never wavered in his Anglicanism, and his trumpet gave forth the not uncertain sound which was needed to convince English Churchmen that their Church was not falling apart but was in travail of rebirth.

Consequences

The Tractarians, as the first-generation Anglo-Catholics,

were by no means ritualists. In such externals as vestments and ornaments they conformed to the established usage of their day. Ritualism, meaning the sedulous cultivation of what was then considered sound catholic ceremonial, would come with the next generation of the movement. To this day when people say of a parish that it is High-Church or Anglo-Catholic they usually mean that it has a comparatively elaborate ritualism in its services. It may be noted here that one of the lasting results of the Catholic Revival was to make Anglicans generally very conscious, often contentiously so, of corporate worship as vital in the life of the Church and the Christian.

The movement had other important consequences. Although most Anglicans would not call themselves Anglo-Catholics, all have been affected by the Catholic Revival in their believing, praying, and worshiping. The holy communion has become the chief service of worship in almost every parish, whether it is simply or ornately celebrated. Such ornaments as altar crosses, candles, frontals, colored stoles, which were once considered desperately popish, are now normal in the most tenaciously Low Church parishes. Monastic communities have been revived. Such catholic devotional practices as fasting before communion are common. Auriculor confession is practiced by many. But all such fruits of the Catholic Revival are secondary to the primary accomplishment of the movement, which was to restore to Anglicanism the vision of the Church as the living body of Christ, whose ministers are of "the apostolic descent" and whose members are of the one true and immortal household of faith which was founded by Jesus Christ. This self-understanding had always been implicit in the Church of England, but it had been almost forgotten by the time that John Keble preached his sermon. Today, the Anglican who is not aware of his Church's catholic character, however he may describe it, is an eccentric.

[1] Charles Williams, *The Descent of the Dove*, 212.

Chapter Twenty-Four

The Lively Victorians

He had been a religious lad before he left school. That is, he had addicted himself to a party in religion, and having done so had received that benefit which most men do who become partisans in such a cause. We are much too apt to look at schism in our church as an unmitigated evil. Moderate schism, if there may be such a thing, at any rate calls attention to the subject, draws in supporters who would otherwise have been inattentive to the matter, and teaches men to think upon religion. How great an amount of good of this description has followed that movement in the Church of England which commenced with the publication of Froude's *Remains!*

Anthony Trollope, in *Barchester Towers* (published in 1857)

When people say that they find the Victorian Age dull, I wonder how recently and how closely they have looked into it. I find the religious controversialists of Victoria's England lively enough even for my taste. In the passage quoted above, Trollope notes that the movement which began with the publication of Froude's *Remains*, the Catholic Revival, stimulated many who had been "inattentive to the matter . . . to think upon religion." It did indeed.

There were other consequences. The Tractarians had asserted as their fundamental tenet that the Church of England, being Christ's own holy society in the realm, may not be reduced to being a mere religious department of state. Its bishops must rule it as accountable only to the

Lord, not to the politicians or to public opinion. They made this essential point very effectively, and one result was a widespread demand for the revival of the Church Convocation which had not met since 1717. The Convocation consists of two bodies, representing Canterbury and York, but in our century the practice of joint sittings of the two bodies has been established. It is a purely clerical assembly. The legislative powers of Convocation have varied with the varying tides of English Church history, but in every age Churchmen with a strong sense of the Church's catholic character have contended that Convocation is the proper ruling organ of the Church of England.

The re-activation of Convocation was resisted from two sides. Many bishops were against it because they felt that they alone, as members of the House of Lords, should rule the Church. From lay quarters came opposition on the ground that the revival of Convocation would increase clericalism. Laymen of this persuasion wanted Parliament to rule the Church. The opposition lost and Convocation was re-activated in 1854.

Ritualism

The Tractarians themselves were not ritualists, but some of their successors of the next generation were; and so what was called ritualism added its fuel to the flames of the "No popery!" uproar.

Two distinct motivating elements went into this original Anglo-Catholic ritualism. The first was concern with eucharistic doctrine. The ritualists were teaching a doctrine of Christ's real presence in the blessed sacrament which required congruous ornaments and practices of reverence. Incense, prostrations, beautiful vestments and altar hangings, lights: such outward and visible means are appropriate to the worship of the king of heaven in his divine beauty of holiness, present upon his altar throne. Such was the doctrinal element in this ritualism of a century ago. But there was another consideration. The Anglo-Catholics who succeeded the Tractarians had a zeal for carrying the Gospel to the poor and neglected folk of the urban slums. The industrial workers in the slums were generally ignorant, and often illiterate. Pious tracts and learned sermons could hardly reach them. The traditional practices of catholic worship and devotion could reach their hearts and change their lives—and did.

Among that generation of ritualists were some men who may well stand high in the company of heaven, for they gave up all and suffered much for Christ. Among the first of these was Charles Lowder (1820–80) of St. Peter's, London Docks. Soon after starting his mission in London's worst slum area, in 1856, he was nearly lynched by a mob infuriated by his "popish" ritualism. In 1866 a plague swept London, and Fr. Lowder, heroically assisted by Dr. Pusey and others, ministered to both the bodies and souls of the afflicted. Other priests who carried on similar heroic ministries in the slums were Robert Dolling (1851–1902) and Arthur Stanton (1839–1913).

By such ministries the Catholic Revival made many friends among the poor. But it made enemies among those who dreaded what seemed to them the Romeward direction of the movement. These people retaliated by resort to law. The Church of England was by law established. A clergyman guilty of engaging in liturgical practices not strictly sanctioned by the Prayer Book rubrics, or by the currently established interpretation thereof, could be prosecuted. Some clergymen were prosecuted and some went to prison. Thus the ultra-protestants, both inside and outside the Church, enjoyed a belated revenge for the persecution of their spiritual fathers by Archbishop Laud two centuries earlier. But as is usual the martyrs triumphed. The end of the matter was, and is, that an extraordinary range of ceremonial practice is allowed within the Church of England and in all the Anglican Churches. Some of the liturgical

"crimes" for which the ritualist martyrs were jailed a century
ago are now done as a matter of course in most Low Church
parishes, as if there had never been any question about
them. Anglican liturgical history is the happiest of all hunt-
ing grounds for the lover of the unlikely but true.

Christian socialism

Evangelicalism had created a social conscience concerning the poor and oppressed, and the Anglo-Catholics had
invaded the slums under the banner of Christ. It remained
now for another group of Churchmen to provide a Christian
critique upon a society in which poverty and inequity could
flourish. This movement called itself Christian socialism. In
its more recent form it came to be known as Christian
liberalism, to make clear that it is in no sense a Marxist
movement.

The founder and pioneer of Christian socialism was
Frederick Denison Maurice (1805–72), one of the most
influential and controversial of Victorian Churchmen. He
had been raised a Unitarian and gradually came to orthodox
theology and the Church. He could not turn his mind away
from the glaring wrongs of a society in which poor people
were in fact the pawns of the rich. His central conviction
was that the world's disorder outside Christ must be made
the world's order in Christ, who is the head not simply of
the Church but of all humanity. This conviction was the
core of Christian socialism. The object of the movement
was to claim the market-place, factory, home, university,
halls of government, all areas of life for Christ. The Christian socialists declared that the Gospel of Christ is a Gospel
of redemption not merely for the souls of the elect in the
life to come but for the whole life and being of all men, in
this life and in the life to come.

Another leading spirit in Christian socialism was Charles
Kingsley (1819–75), whose name is commonly linked with

what has been called "muscular Christianity." He detested
the kind of asceticism enjoined by the Tractarians, such as
clerical celibacy and fasting. Kingsley was more a reformer
than a revolutionist, more crusader than theologian, and
concerned himself with such causes as public sanitation
rather than the radical reconstruction of society. He was
one of the first of the modern Christian liberals.

Maurice and Kingsley were ably assisted by J. M. Ludlow
(1821–1911), who had an expert knowledge of the French
Revolution. He was resolved to bring about revolutionary
changes in England in a peaceful and Christian way. These
three men worked actively with other friends of labor in
promoting unions and legislation favorable to the working
class.

The most eminent Churchman of the age was a layman
and statesman: William Ewart Gladstone (1809–98). A
devout soul from childhood, he had a strong conviction that
the Christian layman has a vocation no less worthy and
exalted than that of the priest. Gladstone became a staunch
believer in the Tractarian principles, but while catholic in
his faith and churchmanship his work as a Christian liberal
in politics was of the kind approved by the Christian socialists. In Gladstone may be seen a working synthesis of Anglo-
Catholic belief with the zeal of Christian liberalism for
building a better society for the children of God, a synthesis
which was to become the standard of Anglicanism at its best
in the modern world.

The Darwinian revolution

In every time of revolutionary scientific advancement
some Christians have faced bravely and constructively the
challenge of the new knowledge. The Church of Victorian
England was not without such servants of truth, and it was
well that it was so, for it was a time of shaking to the
foundations.

As early as 1830, when Lyell's *Principles of Geology* appeared, Christians were forced to re-think their traditional idea that the world had been created in six days' time some 4000 years before Christ. Geological science now demonstrated that the rocks of earth are millions of years old. But the devastating shocker came in 1859, in Darwin's *Origin of Species*. Darwin's theories seemed flatly to contradict the major premises of the Genesis account of creation. Christians, following Genesis, had assumed that God had created all species of creatures separately and independently, "after their kind." Darwin now presented, on the basis of an immense mass of scientifically examined data, the thesis that the differing species had in fact emerged as the result of natural selection. In *The Descent of Man*, published in 1871, he added the principle that man himself is a product of natural selection and gradual evolution, whose progenitor was a creature of the family of anthropoid apes. That seemed to dispose once for all of the doctrine that man was "made in the image of God."

The Christian mind was appalled by these new principles. The Darwinian revolution presented not only a concept of man which seemed irreconcilable with the historic faith but a concept of God that was even more so. "Natural selection" meant "the survival of the fittest" in the struggle for existence; and the fittest was the most powerful and predatory. This, the new science proclaimed, was the very law of life for all creatures upon this earth, man included. If it was true, God's world is a jungle. Where then is the Everlasting Mercy? How can realistic minds believe in the God whose name is love?

A witty defender of tradition like Disraeli could make fun of the new beliefs. Speaking to the Oxford Diocesan Society in 1864, Disraeli uttered a famous *mot*: "The question is this—Is man an ape or an angel? My lord, I am on the side of the angels." But the Darwinian dragon could not be slain with a quip.

Some Churchmen realized that if all truth comes from God, and all truth is ultimately one, Christians have no need to fear new truth of any kind, from any quarter; rather, as servants of the God of truth they must somehow make it their own. A few names in this connection are worthy of everlasting remembrance.

Three men of towering intellect showed their world that one can live by a simple, child-like faith in Jesus Christ while making one's own all truths new and old. These men, all Fellows of Trinity College, Cambridge, and close friends, were Joseph Barber Lightfoot (1828–89), Brooke Foss Westcott (1825–1901), and Fenton John Anthony Hort (1828–92). They differed in gifts and in their ways of going about their task, but they were at one in their resolve to survey the whole ancient and biblical world scientifically, trusting that the Christian faith will always be stronger for finding the strongest possible foundation in history. It was the spirit and faith in which these men undertook their task which helped thoughtful Christians to find their way into the world of new thought without losing their faith.

As the last decade of the 19th century opened the best minds of the Church were at work assimilating the new truths to the ancient faith. Westcott, Hort and Lightfoot were the leaders at Cambridge. At Oxford a group of younger men worked at the same task, collaborating in the symposium volume Lux Mundi, published in 1889. The best known of the contributors was Charles Gore (1853–1932), later to become Bishop of Worcester, Birmingham and Oxford successively. Lux Mundi was subtitled "A Series of Studies in the Religion of the Incarnation" and its declared purpose was "to put the Catholic faith into its right relation to modern intellectual and moral problems." Gore's essay on "The Holy Spirit and Inspiration" was a rather cautiously phrased argument that it is not inconsistent with the catholic faith to accept the results of scientific critical study of the Scriptures. It marked, however, a complete break with the biblical fundamentalism of Dr. Pusey and the Tractarians. What Anglicans today call liberal catholicism was born with Gore's essay in *Lux Mundi*.

The men of the *Lux Mundi* group were disciples of both the Tractarians and the Christian socialists. In and through them was forged a synthesis of catholic faith with progressive social idealism.

Chapter Twenty-Five

The American Church

This Church is far from intending to depart from the Church of England in any essential point of doctrine, discipline, or worship; or further than local circumstances require.

Preface to the American Book of Common Prayer,
Philadelphia, October, 1789

To this day the American Prayer Book, having gone through several revisions, contains the Preface adopted at the 1789 general convention in which the declaration of intention quoted above is made. The Church has kept its pledge of conformity to its English mother Church in doctrine, discipline, and worship; but "local circumstances" in this country have been very different from the beginning, with the result that in such matters as organization, operation, relationship to its community and nation, and concept of its mission the American Church differs greatly from the English Church.

It may be more useful to the reader if in this chapter we deal with the history of the American Church only in very general terms as necessary background for a synoptic view of this Church as it now is.

The American Church formally came into being at the 1789 convention. For a score of years it floundered confusedly, seemingly unable to get moving on the track of its new destiny. A vital turning point occurred in 1811 with the consecration of John Henry Hobart as Bishop of New York and Alexander Griswold as Bishop of the Eastern Diocese, consisting of all New England except Connecticut. These men had, and gave to others, a vision of their Church's calling in the surging young republic, to be not an "establishment" but an apostolic body. Filled with zeal for this mission, truly apostolic men went out into the expanding frontiers to plant the Church. But the affluent and secure Church in the older regions of East and South failed to give anything like adequate support to the westward mission, which explains why the Episcopal Church never became strong in most of rural America. On the foreign missionary front, the Church in the 19th century did much better, establishing vigorous and fruitful missions in China, Japan, and Latin America.

While some American Churches split over the slavery issue, the Episcopal Church suffered only a temporary inner division which soon healed after the end of the Civil War. The dioceses in the seceding states organized themselves as "The Protestant Episcopal Church in the Confederate States of America." However, the general convention of 1862, which met while the war raged, refused to acknowledge the separate existence of the southern dioceses and their names were included in the roll call. Thus no real schism developed even for a moment.

The major issues and tensions among Churchmen in England were reflected in the American Church throughout the 19th century. Bishop Hobart and Bishop Griswold were leaders of the High Church and Low Church elements respectively in the earlier part of the century; it would be misleading to call these elements "parties" or "factions" as they were at that stage. The older High Churchmen stressed the necessity of apostolic ministerial order, through the episcopate, and the centrality of the catholic creeds and sacraments; they were not ritualists. The early Low Churchmen stressed individual conversion and personal piety.

The Oxford movement in England kindled the American high churchmanship into more aggressive life. In the 1840s the General Seminary in New York City became the center of Anglo-Catholic teaching. Now arose the issue of "ritualism" in this country as in England. The ritualism that shocked so many good souls then would shock nobody today. In 1844 the Anglo-Catholic Church of the Advent was founded in Boston. Its rector, the Reverend William Crosswell, so horrified his bishop by preaching in a surplice, using a stone altar, and placing cross and candles on it that his bishop could not bring himself to visit the parish so long as these abominations were visible.

The 1865 convention appointed a committee to curb ritualism.* After several years of bitter controversy the effort to outlaw such "popish" devices as altar crosses and genuflections finally collapsed, and the Church settled down to the normal Anglican policy of leaving such matters to the free choice of the individual and to local parish custom. Some extreme anti-ritualists, led by George Cummins, Assistant Bishop of Kentucky, left the Church to set up their own, known as the Reformed Episcopal Church. Remarkably few Churchmen went along with them. This schismatic body never became a serious rival to the Episcopal Church. It has abandoned most of the Church's historic teachings and is today a sect almost defunct.

The latter half of the 19th century saw the revival of monastic life within Anglicanism. The earliest order to achieve permanent being was the Society of St. John the Evangelist, popularly known as the Cowley Fathers. A young American priest, Charles C. Grafton, who would later become Bishop of Fond du Lac in Wisconsin, helped to establish this community in England in 1865. Eventually the

---

* Author's Note. The Episcopalian who writes these lines wishes to ask a question parenthetically of members of other Churches. When their Churches face a problem, is it an irresistible automatic reflex action to appoint a committee, as it is with the Episcopalians? One churchman who had had enough of this was the late Bishop Irving Peake Johnson of Colorado, who solemnly declared: "God so loved the world that He did not send a committee!"

American Cowley Fathers became an independent community with their mother house at Cambridge, Mass. The
Order of the Holy Cross has an entirely American history.
It was founded in 1884 by James O. S. Huntington, a priest
working in New York's East Side slums. He envisioned a
monastic community ministering to the poor and under-
privileged. The present Holy Cross monastery at West Park
on the Hudson was established in 1904. For many years the
Holy Cross fathers have carried on the Church's mission in
interior Liberia.

The first American order for women was the Community
of St. Mary, founded at New York in 1885. Other well
known orders of nuns of later foundation are the Society of
St. Margaret, the Community of St. John Baptist, the Sister-
hood of the Holy Nativity, the Community of the Trans-
figuration, the Community of the Holy Spirit, and the
Order of St. Anne.

There are Franciscan and Benedictine communities for
men which are ordered by the traditional Rules associated
with those names.

The Anglican religious orders are predominantly active
rather than enclosed, and carry on a variety of ministries,
most notably teaching.

The Broad Churchmen

During the last two decades of the 19th century emerged
the party generally known as the Broad Churchmen or liberals. These men embraced the new principles of biblical
criticism and combined theological modernism with zeal for
applying the Gospel to the needs of men and society. Their
strongest leader was the eloquent Phillips Brooks (1835–
1893), rector of Trinity Church in Boston and later Bishop
of Massachusetts. Another eminent leader was Henry Cod-
man Potter (1835–1908), who as Bishop of New York de-

veloped an effective strategy of Christian attack upon social evils.

Episcopal liberals and evangelicals are commonly confused, but there is an essential difference between them which is well summed up by Bonnell Spencer, O.H.C. Fr. Spencer writes:

The Evangelicals spring from the desire-for-conversion root of the Reformation. In order to preach conversion effectively they must appeal to the emotions on the basis of clear-cut belief that unless one is converted one is damned. The Liberals on the other hand spring from the new-learning root, are vague about doctrine, want no clear-cut distinctions and appeal strictly to the intellect.[1]

There has always been much overlap among these various churchmanship elements and there is more than ever today. Although Episcopalians seem to be, and are, very conscious of what they call churchmanship, most of them would be hard put to classify themselves neatly and definitively.

Although churchmanship tensions are diminishing, the more basic tension between conservative and liberal spirits is not. This conflict is spreading and deepening throughout the American Churches in general. Among Episcopalians it is primarily bound up with the question of what should be the nature and scope of the Church's participation in political and social processes for the reform of society. Clergymen who are "activists" in the civil rights crusade or the anti-war movement devote much of their time, and preaching, to activities which they consider a relevant application of the Gospel to human needs. The conservative Churchman takes his stand on the traditional position that human society as a whole can be changed only as human individuals are changed. The liberal-conservative tension is the dominant one in the Episcopal Church today.

Moreover, this liberal-conservative tension penetrates all areas of concern. The theological, for example: One of the most conspicuous and radical of the "death-of-God" theologians of today is an Episcopal priest, Paul van Buren, author of *The Secular Meaning of the Gospel*. His thesis, *in nuce*, is that all Christian talk about God is essentially talk about man, whether he who speaks is aware of it or not; meaningful talk about God is impossible. Another Episcopal priest, Professor Joseph Fletcher, is a leading spokesman of the situation-ethics school of moralists. Their key principle is that, for Christians, the sole rule of action in any given situation must be what love calls for, to the exclusion of all laws of supposedly universal and unexceptionable applicability. This disposes of the Ten Commandments, among other things.

The most familiar theological disturber of the peace is James A. Pike, resigned Bishop of California, who not only questions but ridicules such venerable doctrines as the Holy Trinity. Bishop Pike is essentially a rationalist who maintains that if a belief is not rationally "plausible" it is not to be held and taught, even if the status of revealed truth is claimed for it. An effort by some of his episcopal colleagues to bring Bishop Pike to a formal trial for heresy in 1967 resulted in a strongly worded statement of censure of his way of expressing his views, but no trial. The affairs created widespread bitterness on both sides, much of which persists.

Those who defend the right of such men to teach their views in the Church argue that it is only by such openness that the Church can stay alive in this age. The orthodox retort is that these men are not simply reformulating the old Gospel but scrapping it and replacing it with new "gospels" of their own devising.

Another matter which absorbs much avid attention by Episcopalians is ecumenism. More will be said about this in a later chapter. Here it may be noted that at the time of this writing, early in 1968, the Episcopal Church is engaged in continuing participation along with nine radically protestant bodies, in the ecumenical venture known as the Consultation on Church Union. At the same time, in many places throughout the land there are friendly meetings and joint worship services between Episcopalians and Roman Catholics. It is safe to say without qualification that since Vatican II there has been an enormous increase of good-will and desire for closer relationship toward the Roman Catholic Church. Still a touchy subject with many Episcopalians is the Roman Church's requirement that in "mixed marriages" the non-Roman party must make concessions concerning the religious upbringing of children which, they feel, no parent should be required to make. But this, and other points of disagreement, are now freely and openly discussed. As of this moment, the most promising ecumenical advances in which the Episcopal Church has figured are on the neighborhood, inter-personal, "grass roots" level.

A revision of the American Prayer Book, for the first time since 1928, is now in the stage of preliminary study. The Church's liturgical commission which is charged with Prayer Book revision (subject to authorization by the general convention) has done something that has never been done before, by drafting a "trial rite" of the eucharist which is now being tried in parishes throughout the Church. The reactions of worshipers to the proposed new liturgy are being collated and will be taken into full account before the final draft is made. This trial rite now in experimental use is no cautious venture, but bold in substance and detail. The initial reaction of many worshipers is one of shock. Recently I have heard an increasing number of expressions of the view that the present time is not auspicious for a revision of the liturgy because it is a time of such theological upheaval and confusion. But because of the constitutional procedures involved in Prayer Book revision it will be at least nine years from now before a new Prayer Book can be officially born. By that time, who knows? In any event, the current trial use is provoking almost all concerned Churchmen to think as they never have before about the words and actions of the Church's corporate worship.

There is a general feeling that the Church has grown too

unwieldly for most effective functioning, and in 1969 a special constitutional convention will be held which will devote itself solely to the task of streamlining and updating the organization of the Church. In principle, the Church is ruled by the general convention, which meets every three years. The general convention approves programs which are administered by the executive council and its staff, of which the Presiding Bishop is the head. All the familiar, safe, sound American "checks and balances" are here. But the ecclesiastical machine grinds cumbersomely and slowly under the heavy load of functionaries "checking and balancing" each other. Much complaining is heard about the "bureaucracy at 815," by which is meant the professional staff of the executive council with headquarters at the Episcopal Church Center, 815 Second Avenue, New York City.

The general convention itself is, in the eyes of many, unmanageably large, and also far from being well representative of the Church membership as a whole. Those who would simplify it urge drastic reduction of its size, and more frequent sessions.

At the 1967 general convention in Seattle a great victory was won for the women of the Church when, after years of controversy, the canons were changed to allow women to serve as members of the house of deputies. Most Episcopalians seem happy, or at least relieved, to have this issue resolved.

Another decision by the 1967 convention is proving much less popular. The Presiding Bishop, the Rt. Rev. John E. Hines, was deeply moved and troubled by the riots in some urban centers in the summer of 1967, and after intense study of the crisis concluded that the Church must lead the way in a whole new kind of ministry. He presuaded the general convention to adopt a program calling for the expenditure of $9 million during the current triennium, in grants to organizations of the urban poor which are striving for greater power in American life. It is presented as a program of helping people to help themselves, in place of the older paternalistic welfare approach. I must record that as of this moment, four months following the authorization and adoption of this program, there is much passive resistance to it throughout the Church. It may be that as the Church's leaders try to explain the purpose and the strategy of the program it will win acceptance. Unless and until it does, the Church will find itself hard pressed for the funds to carry out this program and to carry on its other ministries. The general convention can authorize a program, but unless that program is effectively "sold" to the people who must pay for it the program cannot get off the drawing boards.

*   *   *

This year I observe the 30th anniversary of my ordination to the priesthood. Never in all my ministry do I recall a time when there seemed to be as much heated controversy within the Church as there is today and about so many issues. I cannot report that it is all just good healthy vigorous debate. In the Episcopal Church, as apparently in all the American Churches, there is a growing intensification of the struggle for control between those who may loosely be termed conservatives and liberals. It seems naive to speak of all controversy as good—stimulating, invigorating, and all that. But as I listen to it (and I don't always just listen) being waged by my fellow Churchmen, I find myself reflecting: Never in all these years have I so fully realized that so many Churchmen *care* so deeply about these things they fight about.

On the whole, it is a good feeling, with a strong dash of hope in it.

1 Bonnell Spencer, *Ye Are The Body*, 340.

Chapter Twenty-Six

The Anglican Communion

The Church is . . . Catholic; because it is universal, holding earnestly the Faith for all time, in all countries, and for all people; and is sent to preach the Gospel to the whole world.
Offices of Instruction in the American Book of Common Prayer

The Anglican Communion is not the Church of England writ large and spread over the globe. It is the family of Churches which historically are the children (and grandchildren) of the Church of England and are in communion with Canterbury. It is a common mistake, but a bad one, to say, for example, that the Protestant Episcopal Church USA is the Church of England in the USA. "PECUSA" is not "C of E" but its daughter, living in full independence of its parent.

Clearly the Anglican Communion was never planned by any mortal man. In our survey from the birth of Christianity in Roman Britain to *Lux Mundi* we have seen more than enough of the efforts of sinful men to use the Church of Christ as their own instrument or property. The history of any Church reveals the same sordid human effort. These are the gates of hell striving constantly but vainly to prevail against the Church of Jesus.

Here we may note briefly the first ventures of Anglicanism beyond the borders of England, into the other lands of the British Isles.

To begin with Scotland: In the bloodless revolution of 1688, which replaced James II with William and Mary, the Scottish bishops were forced to take the non-juring position. They could not in good conscience swear allegiance to the new sovereigns. As a result, the Episcopal Church in Scotland was reduced to a minority sect and the Presbyterian Church was established as the Church of Scotland. The non-juring Episcopalians suffered cruel persecution for a hundred years. Their Calvinist Presbyterian countrymen hated them as heartily as they hated Roman Catholics, if not more so. The Scottish Episcopalians, with nothing of worldly gain or privileged status, kept the faith through tribulation and set a high standard for the rest of Anglicanism of unwavering devotion.

It can be plausibly argued that Ireland is predominantly Roman Catholic rather than Anglican today because the Anglican bishops in Ireland in the days of Elizabeth I failed to have a true pastoral care for their Irish people. Certainly they failed to make the most of their opportunity. But the Church of England in Ireland has remained, a small but staunch and solid body. In 1869 the British Parliament disestablished and disendowed the Irish Church. Since then it has been wholly autonomous and independent of England. Its governing body, the general synod, is much like the general convention of the American Church, but is unique in that there are twice as many lay members as clerical. The Irish Anglicans are determined to keep control among the laymen. Another interesting feature is the Irish Church's extreme antiritualism. The celebrant of the eucharist is directed by the rubrics to stand at the north end of the holy table; colored stoles may not be worn; and until 1964 a cross could not be placed on or behind the holy table. Doctrinally, however, the Irish Church is firmly attached to Anglican faith and order.

Like the Irish of Elizabethan times, the Welsh had their own language, were tenaciously devoted to it, and refused to be Anglicized so that they might be Anglicanized. In one

of history's vivid displays of official stupidity the Welsh
Church was ordered by Parliament in 1549 to hold its
services in English. At that time the traditional Latin was
more familiar to most Welshmen than was English. But
whereas the Irish reacted against legally imposed English
services by returning to Roman Catholicism the Welsh reacted by turning to dissent. The Anglican Church in Wales
soon became a minority body, but it was not until 1920 that
it was officially disestablished. Once it became autonomous
it adopted a form of self-government generally like that of
the American Church.

Global expansion

The ventures of Anglicanism into Scotland, Ireland and
Wales were generally inept, but when we look beyond the
British Isles into other climes and continents we find a
brighter picture. In fact, it may be said for the great
Churches of Europe and America in the 19th century that
in no previous age had Christians shown more zeal for going
into all the world to plant the Gospel, and in this zeal the
Anglicans were by no means lacking or lagging. At the very
time when the Church's critics in England were announcing
its sickness unto death the Church overseas was exulting in
growth and expansion in almost every quarter of the globe.
It had become a geographical and political fact that the sun
never set on the king's dominions, and the world-wide
British Empire provided the frame-work for a world-wide
Anglican Communion. To illustrate the growth that took
place in some parts of the Empire: in 1890 there were 200
baptisms in Uganda, in 1940 there were nearly 100,000.

It has become fashionable in our age to decry the close
connection in the last century between western colonialism
and Christian missionary activity. Whatever may be said
against this association, such as it was, we must remember

that in the 19th century the more-or-less Christian nations
had much to give to the under-developed peoples of such
blessings as medical science, education, and social order
beneficial to the individual person. Anybody making an objective study of the modern history of such a nation as India
will see that Christianity has been an immensely liberating
and progressive force in the recreation of a society into its
modern form and ethos. It may be in order, in the interest
of overdue justice, to recall some words of Professor George
Santayana spoken around the turn of this century when the
British Empire was at its zenith. He wrote:

Never since the heroic days of Greece has the world had such a
sweet, just, boyish master. It will be a black day for the human
race when scientific blackguards, conspirators, churls and fanatics
manage to supplant him![1]

He was referring to the imperial Briton, and his words have
proved terribly prophetic. The British master of the world,
who had something of a Christian mind, conscience, and
sense of duty, has been succeeded by such "scientific blackguards, conspirators, churls and fanatics" as Hitler, Tojo,
Stalin and Mao. Who will say that the world is happier in
consequence?

There are several noteworthy characteristics of world
Anglicanism. One is its refusal to engage in proselytism in
other Christian lands. It could be argued that there has been
a major exception to this in some parts of Latin America
where the people are nominally Roman Catholic and the
American Episcopal Church has created and maintained
missions. Those who defend this policy point to the continuing primitive paganism of large masses of the native
peoples despite the long presence of the Roman Catholic
Church in those lands. The Anglican mission as such is to
pagans, not to other Christians.

Another primary fact is that it is always the Church's
hope and purpose to create an independent and autonomous

Church in the mission field, a Church which will be truly of the people, rather than British or American, in its language, ethos, culture, and way of working. The visitor to such an Anglican Church as "The Church of India, Burma and Ceylon" or the "Nippon Sei So Kwai" (The Holy Catholic Church in Japan) will find a fully native Christian community, albeit the product of the missionary effort of Englishmen or Americans. Yet he will find also that the faith, ministry and sacraments of that Church are as Anglican as the Church of England. Anglicanism is not "Englishness" in religion, at least in modern times. The emancipation of world Anglicanism from bondage to Anglo-Saxon cultural domination really began with the consecration of an Indian, V. S. Azariah, as Bishop of Dornakal in 1912. Many English Churchmen viewed this step with paternalistic alarm, feeling that only an English episcopate could rule the Church in a predominantly non-Christian land. Bishop Azariah proved them wrong, and it quickly became general Anglican policy to train native men for the ministry and leadership of the "younger Churches" as fast as possible.

The Lambeth Conferences

The Anglican Communion is a loosely organized, voluntary family of sister Churches. It has no over-arching central authority corresponding to the Vatican. Its bond of unity is a common ministry, creed, liturgy, and historical descent from the See of Canterbury. The Anglican Churches are entirely local in their relationships to their respective states, in their forms of self-administration, in their languages and customs. The replacement of diversity by uniformity in such matters has never been desired. But it became clear during the age of world-wide expansion in the 19th century that, lacking anything like the Vatican, the Anglican Communion needed some means of expressing and implementing its real unity. Out of this grew the Lambeth Conference. It first met in 1867 at Lambeth, which for six centuries has been the London residence of the Archbishops of Canterbury. These conferences are attended by Anglican bishops from throughout the world, and they meet about once in every ten years.

Lambeth has no legislative or jurisdictional authority whatever. It serves solely as an organ of episcopal opinion on problems confronting the Church. Its judgments are expressed in formal reports which are published immediately following each conference. Although the authority of Lambeth is purely moral and advisory it is none the less very great. Lambeth pronouncements on such subjects as Christian reunion, war, race relations and all other moral problems confronting man and society are generally accepted as speaking the mind of the Church.

Anglican Congresses

The Lambeth Conferences are attended only by bishops. In recent years there has developed a sense of need for another kind of pan-Anglican deliberative body, to be made up of bishops, clergy and laity. The result is the Anglican Congress, which met in Minneapolis in 1954. It met again in Toronto in 1963. Like Lambeth, the Congresses are strictly deliberative in nature, producing reports and findings which carry much moral weight with the Church at large. Perhaps more important in ultimate effect is the way in which the Anglican Congresses impress upon those attending them the remarkable universality of their Church and Communion as they meet with delegates representing all climes and kindreds of earth. Nowhere is the Anglican achievement of a free and

uncoerced unity in essentials amid diversity in non-essentials
more dramatically proclaimed than by these Congresses.

[1] This remark of Santayana's is quoted without source by S. E. Mori-
son, *The Oxford History of the American People*, 139.

Chapter Twenty-Seven

Anglicanism and Reunion

The times call us to a new outlook and new measures. The Faith cannot be adequately apprehended and the battle of the Kingdom cannot be worthily fought while the body is divided, and is thus unable to grow up into the fullness of the life of Christ. The time has come, we believe, for all the separated groups of Christians to agree in forgetting the things that are behind and reaching out towards the goal of a reunited Catholic Church. The removal of the barriers that have arisen between them will only be brought about by a new comradeship of those whose faces are definitely set this way.

From the letter *To all Christian People* from the Lambeth Conference of 1920.

Most Christians who think earnestly about the tasks and problems of Christian reunion look to the Anglican Churches to play a unique role in the process of reconciling the catholic and the reformational elements in modern Christendom. Within Anglicanism itself there has developed a sense of this special vocation.

In the early chapters of our historical survey we saw how the young Church in Britain realized its insufficiency all by itself and had to draw strength from the rest of the body. It may be said that the Anglican Communion as we know it today inherits this sense of incompleteness within itself, with the longing implicit in that sense for the completeness of reunion and restoration of the wholeness of the Church.

We have seen enough of the English Church's conflicts with Rome on one side and the Calvinist sectaries on the other, in the 16th and 17th centuries, to explain why it was that for a long time any thought of *rapprochement* with either adversary was impossible. The first noteworthy ecumenical motions came in the 18th century, and the first noteworthy name in this movement is that of William Wake (1657–1737), who became Archbishop of Canterbury in 1716. In 1682 he had gone to Paris as chaplain to the English ambassador and there he became acquainted with Gallicanism. Later, as Archbishop of Canterbury, he discussed reunion with representatives of the French Church. Wake equally appreciated both catholic and protestant traditions and reached out to both Roman Catholics and dissenters. He helped to formulate a plan to unite the Lutherans and Calvinists in Prussia on the basis of episcopacy and the English Prayer Book translated into German. Of course it didn't work. Wake was born two centuries too early for his ideas and hopes, but his witness did not fall fruitless to the ground.

Ecumenical relations between Anglicanism and Eastern Orthodoxy began in the 18th century. In 1701 the Archbishop of Philippopolis visited England, and a few years later so did the Armenian patriarch. These prelates were courteously received by the English Church leaders but there is no record of any formal discussion of the barriers separating their Churches. In 1716 the non-juring bishops approached the Church of Russia hoping to find some basis for union or for close relations. They failed, partly at least because they obviously did not represent the Church of England as a whole.

The Catholic Revival in the 19th century made some English Churchmen more sympathetically conscious of the Roman and Eastern Churches, but there were two stiffly inhibiting factors. One was the remoteness and strangeness of

Eastern Orthodoxy to most Englishmen. The other was the old political suspicion and distrust of Rome which lingered. Newman in his Anglican days had taught that the pope was Antichrist. In a later generation, however, a friendlier spirit toward Rome was born in some Churchmen, most notably in the devout layman, Lord Halifax, who devoted himself wholeheartedly to the cause of reunion between England and Rome. In 1894 he became acquainted with a French priest, the abbé Portal, and they initiated Anglican-Roman conversations which went on for two years. But this effort, which seemed promising for a while, was halted by Pope Leo XIII's bull *Apostolicae Curae* in the fall of 1896. The bull condemned Anglican orders as invalid through defect of form and intention. The next year the two English Archbishops issued a *Responsio,* and from that time to the present the issue has been an open one. But for the time being, after the issuance of *Apostolicae Curae,* further discussion between the two Churches seemed futile.

The modern *entente cordiale* between the Anglican and Orthodox Churches began with William Palmer's visit to Russia in 1850. So enamored was this High Churchman of the glories of Orthodoxy, and so disenchanted by the persecution of Anglo-Catholics in his own Church, that he seriously considered joining the Orthodox; eventually however he became a Roman Catholic. John Mason Neale (1818–66) did much to stimulate Anglican appreciation of Orthodoxy through his translations of Eastern hymns and his historical studies.

From the time when the body known as the Old Catholics seceded from Rome in 1870, refusing to accept papal infallibility, the Anglicans have been interested in them, and in 1922 the two Churches were brought into full intercommunion.

The Lambeth Conference of 1878 expressed a hope for closer relationships with the Scandinavian Churches, especially the Church of Sweden. The Swedish Church has preserved the historic episcopal succession, so the usual problem

of the ministry does not stand in the way. In 1920 a relationship of qualified intercommunion was formally established
between the English and Swedish Churches.

In 1931 the Bonn Agreement between the Church of
England and the Old Catholics declared that each Communion recognized the catholicity and independence of the
other and that members of each might receive the sacraments in the other. It proclaimed that

intercommunion does not require from either communion the
acceptance of all doctrinal opinion, sacramental devotion, or
liturgical practice characteristic of the other, but implies that
each believes the other to hold all the essentials of the Christian
faith.

In 1946, the Polish National Catholic Church and the American Episcopal Church established intercommunion on the
basis of the Bonn Agreement.

In the Philippines, a group of some 20 priests and more
than a million laity broke from the Roman Catholic Church
in 1920 and became the Philippine Independent Church.
They wanted to remain catholic in doctrine, liturgy and
order, but they had no bishops. They appealed to the
Episcopal Church to provide consecration. In 1948 three
Episcopal bishops consecrated three PIC priests as bishops.
Full intercommunion between the two Churches was established in 1961.

Thus far, all the solid successes achieved by the Anglican
Churches in their ecumenical outreach, resulting in intercommunion or mutual acceptance of ministries, have been
with essentially catholic bodies. The Church of Sweden is
Lutheran in doctrine but has retained the catholic ministry
and creeds. Anglican efforts to achieve similar results with
protestant bodies have failed. Between 1937 and 1946 the
Episcopal and Presbyterian Churches in America engaged
in intensive negotiation directed toward organic union, but
finally had to abandon the project. At that time many Episcopalians felt that the proposed reunion formula did not

meet the conditions of the Lambeth Quadrilateral, and to this key document—virtually the constitution—of Anglican ecumenism we now turn our attention.

The Lambeth Quadrilateral, issued by the Lambeth Conference of 1888, is a slightly revised version of a statement issued by the American Church's general convention in 1886. It declares the four requisites for a reunited Church to be the following:

A. The Holy Scriptures of the Old and New Testament, as "containing all things necessary to salvation," and as being the rule and ultimate standard of faith.

B. The Apostles' Creed, as the Baptismal Symbol; and the Nicene Creed, as the sufficient statement of the Christian Faith.

C. The two Sacraments ordained by Christ Himself—Baptism and the Supper of the Lord—ministered with unfailing use of Christ's Words of Institution, and of the elements ordained by Him.

D. The Historic Episcopate, locally adapted in the methods of its administration to the varying needs of the nations and peoples called of God into the Unity of His Church.

Practically from the moment of its formulation the Quadrilateral has been the map and the basis for Anglican ecumenical effort, and only by some major revolution in the character of Anglicanism itself could it conceivably be repudiated. In all negotiations and discussions to date between Anglicans and various protestant bodies it has been the second and fourth points of the Quadrilateral, the positions on the catholic creeds and the episcopate, which have presented roadblocks.

At the time of this writing (1968) the Church of England is holding conversations with the Methodists and the Roman Catholics, and in America the Episcopal Church is participating in the Consultation on Church Union. All the other participants in the Consultation are of the reformed protestant traditions; there are no Lutheran or catholic bodies among them. This, however, may change at any time.

Anglicans have a special interest in the Church of South

India, which is the only successful achievement to date of
organic union of episcopal and non-episcopal bodies. The
CSI came into being in 1947 by the union of the South India
United Church, the Methodist Church in South India, and
the four southern dioceses of the Anglican Church of India,
Pakistan, Burma and Ceylon. These four dioceses left the
Anglican Communion in order to bring the episcopate to
the new CSI. The Church now ordains all its clergy episcopally. It is based doctrinally upon the Lambeth Quadrilateral and claims to be a fully catholic Church in which
some congregational, presbyterian and episcopal elements
are preserved. Many Anglicans, however, are troubled by
some parts of the constitution of the CSI. In the Nandyal
district of South India some 40,000 Anglicans refused to
join the Church of South India and remain to this day in
the Anglican Communion, in an awkward and anomalous
position.

There seems to be less talk than in earlier years in ecumenical discussion about Anglicanism as a "bridge" between
catholicism and protestantism. The bridge metaphor suggests that the Roman Catholic from one side and the Presbyterian or Lutheran from the other might both make use
of the convenient Anglican bridge as a means of meeting,
since this bridge presumably reaches both shores. The metaphor seems due for some revision or restatement. In practice,
the "separated brethren" are not using the Anglican bridge
as a place to meet each other, and it is hard to see why they
should or how they could. The Roman Catholic and the
Lutheran Churches are engaged in direct ecumenical
conversation today—quite independently of the Anglican
"bridge."

A growing number of Anglicans see the future ecumenical
role of their Church as something quite different. They agree
with the Roman Catholic ecumenical scholar William H.
van de Pol. Noting the emergence in Anglicanism since
World War II of a dominant movement toward a "central
churchmanship" which is a genuine blending of the older

Anglo-Catholic, evangelical and liberal elements, he predicts:

The more the moderate type of Anglicanism of "central churchmanship" develops, the more the Anglican Communion will grow in the direction of a prototype of reunited Christianity, and be recognized as such by the other Churches.[1]

I, for one, am sure this is true.

[1] William H. van de Pol, *Anglicanism in Ecumenical Perspective*, 98. American edition, Duquesne University Press.

Chapter Twenty-Eight

Today and Tomorrow

The genius of the Anglican inheritance is experiment working upon tradition.

F. R. Barry

One cannot speak of today and tomorrow as an historian but only as an observer of things present, and as a predicter of, and guesser about, things to come. I find however that I cannot end this book without expressing my own assessment of the present and expectation of the future of Anglicanism.

To begin with a synoptic view of the Anglican Communion as it is, its 20 autonomous Churches are the following, in their historical order of appearance:

1. The Church of England.
2. The Church in Wales.
3. The Church of Ireland.
4. The Episcopal Church in Scotland.
5. The Protestant Episcopal Church in the U.S.A.
6. The Anglican Church of Canada.
7. The Church of India, Pakistan, Burma and Ceylon.
8. The Church of England in Australia.
9. The Church of the Province of New Zealand.
10. The Church of the Province of South Africa.
11. The Church of the Province of the West Indies.
12. Nippon Seikokai (Holy Catholic Church of Japan).

13. Chung Hua Sheng Kung Hui (Holy Catholic Church of China).
14. The Church of the Province of West Africa.
15. The Church of the Province of Central Africa.
16. The Archbishopric in Jerusalem.
17. The Church of the Province of East Africa.
18. The Church of the Province of Uganda.
19. Iglesia Episcopal Brasileira (The Episcopal Church of Brazil).
20. Extra-provincial dioceses holding mission from the See of Canterbury (Argentina and Eastern South America with the Falkland Islands, Bermuda, Chile with Bolivia and Peru, Gibraltar, Jesselton, Korea, Kuching, Madagascar, Mauritius, North Africa, Seoul, and Singapore and Malaya).

The total membership of baptized persons is approximately 46 million. The largest of the Anglican Churches in formal membership is the Church of England, listing some 27 million. The American and Australian Church, each with about 3½ million members, come next in size.

These statistics simply by themselves tell us nothing about where the Church is gaining and where it is losing. The Church of England has been seriously losing in membership and active communicant strength since World War II. As was the case somewhat more than a century ago, there is little aggressive hostility to the Church in England, still less to Christianity as a faith and religion. There is much indifference, born of a spiritual weariness and a feeling that the Church, like some other venerable English institutions, has outlived its usefulness. The situation of the Church of England is essentially that of the historic European Churches in general, such as the Roman Catholic Church in France or Italy, or the Lutheran Church in Sweden or Germany. These Churches exist in societies which are increasingly secular, and post-Christian.

Stephen Neill wrote in 1958:

The situation of Anglicanism in England is perhaps more problematic than it is in other countries. Almost everywhere else it shows a vigour and a hopefulness, from which the Church of England has much to learn. Over most of the world, numerical progress is sedate and gradual. But, if we wish to grasp the significance of the present hour and of the present challenge to the Anglican Churches, it is to Africa that we must turn. Here progress is sensational . . .[1]

He goes on to cite the growth statistics of the Church in Africa, and they do indeed reflect sensational progress in conversions. Today, nine years after Neill made this observation, the Church's growth in Africa is proceeding almost as rapidly.

In the same book, written in 1958, Bishop Neill commented on the Episcopal Church in America:

Some observers comment on the superficiality of American religion, on the dominance of social custom, which almost requires membership in a Church as a certificate of respectability, on the ease with which Americans pass from denomination to denomination, on the profound inner anxiety which is the counterpart of teeming prosperity, and which seeks an anodyne in religious feeling. When full allowance has been made for all this, American religion is still one of the most remarkable phenomena in the contemporary world; and the most skilled observers are more impressed by the steady deepening, the increased seriousness of American religious convictions, than they are dismayed by what still remains of its traditional superficiality. The Protestant Episcopal Church manages to maintain one priest for every four hundred members, and pays its clergy reasonably well. Churches are crowded; services are conducted briskly but reverently. To a discouraged English Anglican, to preach in any of the great churches of the American Episcopal Church is a heartening and a gladdening experience.[2]

When Bishop Neill made this good report on the American Church this country was still in the "religious boom" which followed the war. Strangely, the British Churches experienced "bust" rather than "boom" during those years.

Today, in 1968, the post-war religious boom in America is a thing of the past. Church services are still generally well attended. A substantial majority of Americans claim some definite religious affiliation. But the traditional American insistence upon church membership as "a certificate of respectability" is noticeably waning. There is still much said and written about the Episcopal Church as the prime ecclesiastical club for the social climbers and the status seekers, but this has never been as generally true as the legend suggests and it seems to be well on the way out.

There is today a strong drive throughout the Anglican Communion toward a stronger pan-Anglican unification. Anglicans cherish individual freedom and, as an extension of this, provincial freedom in the form of self-rule and self-determination by each member Church. There is deep-rooted resistance to regimenting authority and autocratic central government. But as Churchmen in their respective areas and provinces become more aware of each other their sense of unity in a worldwide fellowship of shared faith and life grows. The Lambeth Conferences and more recently the Anglican Congresses have powerfully stimulated this growth. It seems quite inevitable that in the years ahead the Anglican Communion will become more unified in organization, strategy and operation throughout the world.

"The genius of the Anglican inheritance is experiment working upon tradition," says Bishop F. R. Barry of the Church of England. I hope that the truth of this has been amply demonstrated in the preceding chapters of this book. The tradition is that of the historic catholic Church, in faith, ministry, mission and worship. At all times, this sacred deposit stands in peculiar jeopardy within the Anglican Communion, because the Anglican "process" is experiment working upon the tradition. This Church puts up with a great deal which some other Churches would never tolerate, all in the hope that the "experiment" of the moment will somehow in the end serve the tradition. Anglicanism's extraordinary patience with "experimenters" is most vividly revealed in the realm of doctrine. Within recent years an English bishop has proposed dropping the concept of God as our Father in heaven and replacing it with a properly demythologized concept of God as the Ground of all being; and an American bishop dismisses the Holy Trinity as a "committee-God." Neither of these prelates, Robinson of England or Pike of America, would last long in the Roman Catholic or Orthodox or Lutheran Church. Wisely or unwisely, the Anglican Communion endures much of this sort of thing on its principle of experiment working upon tradition and in its hope that God will make the errors and excesses of men to turn to his praise.

What normally happens is that the experimenter or reviser comes along, has his say, provokes a furious general row, goes his way, and the Church gets back to where it was —but not quite. An example is that of the Victorian ritualists who defied the established order to place crosses and lights on altars, to wear colored stoles, to bow at the name of Jesus, and to practice auricular confession. Some of them got rough treatment indeed for their audacious experimenting. But in the final issue the Church found itself accepting much that the rebels had fought for, as a matter of course. Today some of the Church's moral theologians are boldly advocating what is called situation ethics, in which only love, never law, is to determine one's behavior in any situation. What will come of this at last? So long as the old pattern still operates, it is predictable that tradition will prevail— but with a difference. There will not be a return to a simple moral legalism. Churchmen will realize in principle and in practice more clearly than they did before that, as St. Paul taught long ago, Christians are to "owe no man anything, but to love one another." (Romans 13:8)

Too many students of Anglicanism, it seems to me, think of it too exclusively in terms of its ecumenical role and vocation. A few years ago an eminent Churchman said that the vocation of the Anglican Communion is to disappear, and this has become something of a proverb. I consider it dangerously misleading and I reject it. There is a profound spiritual sense in which it is the vocation of any Church, like any Christian person, to die to self in the service of God's will and purpose. This however is not what those who make of this slogan their golden text have in mind. They evidently think that if ever this Church has an opportunity to make possible a union of Churches by entering a merger and voting itself institutionally out of existence it should do so. As I (and many other Anglicans) see it, this would not be a Christian dying to self; it would be corporate suicide.

There are two distinct ways of viewing the Anglican ecumenical vocation. One is to see Anglicanism as a temporary institution or movement which God provides solely for the accomplishment of the reunion of Christendom. The other is to see it, in van de Pol's phrase quoted in the last chapter, as "a prototype of reunited Christianity." If the Anglican Communion is to serve as such a prototype, it must keep itself alive and intact to fulfil this purpose.

Anybody who has read this book thus far has seen all manner of frailty, fault and ineptitude in the past and present life of the Anglican Communion. I have tried to emulate Oliver Cromwell, who charged his portrait painter: "Paint me as I am, warts and all!" Anglicanism is by no means wartless. A Church without warts—or, in scriptural language, "not having spot, or wrinkle" (Ephesians 5:27)— would be, not the Church Militant still in its pilgrimage, but the Church Triumphant in its eternal and glorious end. What can be said for the Anglican Communion is that it demonstrates something of inestimable value and importance to the people of God: that the Church can be "truly catholic, truly evangelical, and truly reformed"[3] without bursting asunder like the poor chameleon set on a piece of plaid. The Roman Catholic Church today is working toward a new freedom for the individual within the household of faith. The Anglican individual has had this freedom for centuries. Many protestants are reaching for a fuller sacramental life, and a stronger hold on the historic apostolic faith of

Christendom, while at the same time insisting upon having these treasures without returning to ecclesiastical bondage. Here again, the Anglican synthesis shows that these treasures can be had, in freedom.

To be this laboratory of experiment working upon tradition, this prototype of a reunited Christianity, is a large part of the vocation of Anglicanism for today and tomorrow. God will use it in his own way for the healing of the divisions in the body of Christ. But it is also a home for souls, a living portion of the Church in which the Good Shepherd feeds his people with the Bread of Life.

[1] Stephen Neill, *Anglicanism*, 411.
[2] *Ibid*, 410.
[3] This phrase is in a sense the working text of the Consultation on Church Union as it envisions the united Church of the future. The participants in the Consultation hold that the Church of God can never be less than "truly catholic, truly evangelical, and truly reformed."

Appendix

A non-Anglican friend who was kind enough to read this book in manuscript complained whimsically that for all its considerable bulk it didn't answer all of his questions. I asked him to set down the questions which, in his judgment, a thoughtful person standing outside the Anglican Communion might still want the answers to, after reading this book as it now stands. He gave me some, and I have added others suggested by my own experience with inquirers and students.

* * *

Explain the position of the Presiding Bishop of the American Episcopal Church. Why isn't he called an archbishop, as in other Anglican Churches?

The Presiding Bishop is the Church's chief executive. He is elected by the house of bishops and must be approved by the house of deputies of the general convention. When he becomes Presiding Bishop he relinquishes his diocesan jurisdiction. He is not called an archbishop for the reason that he isn't one. An archbishop has governing jurisdiction over other bishops within his province. The Presiding Bishop has no such power. American Episcopalians, largely because they are Americans, have guarded against an office of supra-bishop, for the familiar American reasoning about the concentration of power in the hands of any individual.

What is the system of clergy placement in the Episcopal Church?

The rector of a parish is called by the vestry of that parish. (The vestry is made up of lay people elected by the members of the parish.) The man called by the vestry must, normally, be approved by the bishop. If the congregation is not a parish but a mission, the priest in charge is appointed by the bishop.

How are bishops chosen?

The bishop of a diocese is elected by a convention of clergy and laity of that diocese. His election must be ratified by most of the other dioceses of the Church, expressing their assent or dissent through their bishops and standing committees. (The standing committee of a diocese is the bishop's council of advice and consent.) The bishop of a missionary jurisdiction, however, is appointed by the house of bishops, ratified by the house of deputies.

What is the Anglican position, both doctrinally and devotionally, concerning the Blessed Virgin Mary?

In the Anglican system, nothing can be taught as necessary dogma unless it can be "proved"—substantiated—by holy Scripture. Therefore, an extra-scriptural opinion about Mary might be held as a private opinion, but not taught as church doctrine. That Mary was blessed among women because she was chosen by God to be the mother of his Son is the fundamental "Anglican position" because it is the fundamental New Testament position. It was an Anglican poet, Wordsworth, who hailed Mary as "our tainted nature's solitary boast." The doctrinal position is that she is to be revered as God's chosen human vessel through whom the divine gift of the Redeemer was given. Mary's "Be it unto me" is the prototype of all Christian obedience.

Many Anglican churches are dedicated to St. Mary the Virgin. She is liturgically commemorated on the Feasts of the Purification and the Annunciation. Some Anglicans use the *Hail Mary* in their private devotions.

In what sense, if any, could Anglicans accept the primacy of the Bishop of Rome, in a re-united Church?

To be quite honest, there are some Anglicans who would answer this question with a ringing and robust *Never!* But they are a small minority. The Archbishop of Canterbury has recently expressed what is undoubtedly the view of a large majority of Anglicans, namely, that there is no reason in the Anglican ecclesiology why the Bishop of Rome, as occupant of the oldest extant see in Christendom, should not be accorded a primacy of honor among the bishops. He could be the re-united Church's presiding officer. He could be the Church's official spokesman; indeed, his office could be the expressive and transmissive organ through which the Church speaks its corporate mind and will to the world. After all, this would be a case of the Church speaking through the pope, not of the pope speaking through the Church. I have read apologetical statements about the papacy, from the Roman side, which seem to define the office in essentially these terms. I see no reason why, as the two Churches draw closer together and seek further guidance from the Holy Spirit, they should not come in the end to a true meeting of minds on this issue.

How can you justify the Episcopal Church's tolerance of men in its ministry, even bishops, who openly question or deny the doctrines which are plainly set forth in the Book of Common Prayer?

I cannot, and so shall not try. I believe such tolerance is a mistake. I know the good intention behind the mistake,

which is to keep the Church open to new visions and appre-
hensions of God's truth. Any good Christian must be for
that. But there is a difference between denying a doctrine
and seeking a deeper understanding of it. For example, if a
man says that the most important thing about the Virgin
Birth is not the miracle of it but the meaning of it, he is not
denying the doctrine at all. But the moment he says "It
didn't happen, as a miraculous event or anything else!" he
should resign his ministerial office, if he has one, for he is
denying that which he has been ordained to teach (among
many other things, of course).

What is the authority of the Articles of Religion in the Church today?

In chapter 13 we considered the original purpose of the
Articles, which was that of setting broad but real limits
upon the range of permissible belief within the Church.
That purpose remains. Today, as in the days of Elizabeth I,
if a Churchman went beyond the Articles toward Rome on
one side, or beyond them toward Geneva on the other side,
he would know from the testimony of the Articles that he
really has stepped outside Anglicanism. But it will be left
to him to be the judge. The Church makes no effort to enforce conformity to the Articles. They are printed with the
Prayer Book for the guidance and information of the faithful. I think there is much more good solid theology contained in at least some of the Articles than is generally
acknowledged. But their "authority" is limited, and essentially negative. It is easier to learn from the Articles what is
not church doctrine than to learn what is.

Who have been the most influential Anglican theologians in modern times?

By "modern times" I assume that what is meant is, say, the

past fifty years. I would answer: in England, William Temple, Charles Gore, Arthur M. Ramsey (present Archbishop of Canterbury), W. R. Inge, Kenneth Kirk and Dom Gregory Dix. In America, among the men who have had the deepest theological influence are William P. Du Bose, Francis J. Hall, Frederick C. Grant, and the liturgical scholar, Massey H. Shepherd. It is not to be denied that two contemporary Churchmen of strongly anti-orthodox convictions, Bishop John Robinson in England and Bishop James Pike in America, are widely influential, whatever one may think of the merits of their influence.

There seems to be a lot of confusion and disagreement among Anglicans about "open communion." What is the inside story on this?

Your observation about the confusion and disagreement is correct. The Episcopal Church, like all Anglican Churches, prescribes baptism and confirmation as pre-requisite to full communicant status as members. The privilege of communion is surely "open" to all persons willing to receive it on these terms, and so I reject the term "closed communion" as descriptive of the formal Anglican policy.

When Christians who are not confirmed members of the Church feel moved by the Holy Spirit to receive the sacrament, they are welcomed at the altar. But it is the feeling of many Episcopalians, perhaps most, that some clergy who go out of their way to urge unconfirmed persons to receive, without making any effort to prepare them for a proper understanding of this holy mystery, are abusing the freedom of their pastoral office. This is what most of the confusion and disagreement is about. The terms "open communion" and "closed communion" as generally used are both misleading.

Since Methodism really began within the Church of England, is there a good prospect of re-union between these two bodies?

That is a consummation devoutly to be wished. At the present time the Anglicans and Methodists in Great Britain are working resolutely toward a viable relation of intercommunion having corporate re-union as the goal. The big problem is that of the ministry, because (as we observed in chapter 21), the Methodists abandoned the historic episcopate. Methodism has had its own corporate life and experience for nearly two hundred years, and in many ways has grown into a different kind of body from its Anglican "mother." But there are signs of promise. Among Anglicans, many feel the need for the evangelical spirit and zeal which they hope they might get from closer fellowship with the Methodists. Likewise, a growing number of Methodists want the beauty and order of the Prayer Book worship and a stronger sacramental life, such as they see in Anglicanism.

What is the position of sacramental confession in Anglicanism?

That the priest at his ordination receives authority to absolve the penitent from sin is made explicit in the ordination rite. He hears confessions and pronounces absolution primarily as part of his pastoral office. There is no canonical requirement to make one's confession to a priest. The familiar Anglican practice and precept is summed up in the saying that sacramental confession is "open to all, commended to some, required of none."

Has the Episcopal Church a definite teaching on the subject of marriage and divorce, and if it has why does there seem to be such a variety of practice?

The Church's teaching, expressed in the Form of Solemnization of Matrimony in the Book of Common Prayer, is as definite as any teaching can be. The man and wife take one another "for better for worse, for richer for poorer, in sickness and in health, to love and to cherish, till death us do part." The indissolubility of a true marital union is taught. Only the death of one partner releases the other from this bond. Such is the teaching of the Church.

The "variety of practice" presumably refers to the fact that some Episcopalians have divorced and married again. Sometimes the civil divorce is accompanied by an ecclesiastical decree of nullity in which it is declared, on evidence, that the original marriage was not a true marriage because it failed to meet the tests of a valid union. Sometimes the clergy are either ignorant of the facts concerning somebody's previous marriage, or are careless about facing what can be a painful pastoral problem. But most often in such cases the couple, one or both of whom have ex-spouses still living, have been married outside the Church, and have been re-admitted to communicant membership in good standing after a period of excommunication, during which time they have given evidence of a firm intention that their present marriage will be a Christian one.

Is the ministry of healing carried on in the Episcopal Church?

Yes, and increasingly so. More and more parishes have special weekly healing services, and the clergy use holy unction regularly in ministering to the sick.

Where does the Episcopal Church stand on the question of birth control?

This is regarded as a matter for the individual conscience to decide. Episcopalians are taught that it is sinful to enter marriage with an intention to avoid having children because one doesn't wish to be bothered with responsibility for them. Birth control can be used purely selfishly, and, when it is, the act is sinful. But it is the selfish intent which is the sin— not the use of contraception.

Why do Episcopalians make so much more of confirmation than do most other Churches?

The whole question of the relation of confirmation to baptism is being thoroughly reconsidered throughout the Anglican Communion. But to answer the question in terms of the past and present: In the Anglican Churches, confirmation is a kind of coming-of-age rite. The candidate has been fully instructed in the fundamentals of the faith. If he was baptized as an infant he made his vows of commitment to the obedience of Christ involuntarily, through his sponsors. Now, in confirmation, he is given a chance to ratify and renew these vows by his own choice. The laying on of hands by the bishop, with prayer, is an ordination of the confirmand to the ministry of the laity. The typical Churchman recalls his own confirmation as one of the great decisive moments in his life with God.

Why is it that a distinction is made between people coming into the Episcopal Church from other bodies, between Catholics—Roman or Orthodox—and Protestants?

The only distinction is that if the former have already been confirmed in their respective communions there is no need for them to be confirmed in the Episcopal Church, since they have already had episcopal confirmation. Such persons are formally received rather than confirmed, to avoid repeating a sacrament which is in the category of sacraments through which "indelible character" is bestowed.

What is the position of Anglican thinking about the question of the ordination of women, which is coming increasingly to the fore in ecumenical discussion?

Anglicans, along with other Christians, are becoming more aware of the problem. Recently a Churchwoman who is strongly opposed to the ordination of women put forth a kind of argument from analogy: that God himself "discriminates" between the sexes by assigning to each sex some wonderful and sacred function which cannot be performed by the others. "If I as a woman cannot be a priest," said she in effect, "neither can my priest as a man be a mother." I suspect that as of now most Episcopalians of either sect would agree with her argument as at least part of their reason for opposing the ordination of women. But the theologians who are speaking out on the subject are most of them saying that they can find no strictly theological reason for holding that women cannot receive holy orders. The present thinking is that it would be radically inexpedient at this time to depart from the traditional policy and practice. But Anglican thinking about the issue, on theoretical grounds, is in flux.

Is there anything that distinguishes Anglican belief from traditional catholic belief about eschatology and the last things?

No, not fundamentally. The realities of death, judgment, hell, and heaven are in various ways recognized and expressed in the Church's liturgy. It should always be remembered that in Anglicanism the law of praying is the law of believing. The "Romish doctrine of purgatory" is explicitly rejected in Article 22, but by this is meant the late medieval doctrine that the passage of souls from purgatory to heaven can be expedited by masses offered on earth. Anglicans pray for the souls of the departed that they may grow in God's love and service, thus expressing their belief in what they prefer to call paradise, or the intermediate state, as an experience of preparation for the fullness of the beatific vision in heaven.

Bibliography

The following list is by no means exhaustive. It includes books which have been useful to the author of this study, and others which are commendable sources of information about Anglicanism. The books are arranged, in general, in chronological or period order.

CHURCHILL, WINSTON. *A History of the English Speaking Peoples.* New York: Dodd, Mead & Co., 1956.

BLAIR, PETER HUNTER. *Roman Britain and Early England.* New York: W.W. Norton & Co., 1962.

WALKER, WILLISTON. *A History of the Christian Church.* New York: Charles Scribner's Sons, 1918, 1945.

MAUROIS, ANDRE. *The Miracle of England.* New York: Harper & Row, 1937.

GODFREY, JOHN. *The Church of Anglo-Saxon England.* Cambridge: Cambridge University Press, 1962.

BEDE. *The Ecclesiastical History of the English Nation.* ("Everyman's Library") New York: E. P. Dutton.

MOORMAN, JOHN R. H. *A History of the Church in England.* New York: Morehouse-Barlow, 1954.

BETTENSON, HENRY (ed.). *Documents of the Christian Church.* New York: Oxford Press, 1947.

NEILL, STEPHEN. *Anglicanism.* (3rd ed.). Baltimore: Penguin Books, 1965.

INGE, W. R. *England.* New York: McGraw-Hill, 1953.

BRYANT, SIR ARTHUR. *Makers of England.* Garden City: Doubleday and Co., 1962.

DURANT, WILL. *The Age of Faith.* New York: Simon and Schuster, 1950.

COULTON, G. G. *Medieval Panorama.* Cambridge: Cambridge University Press, 1937.

POOLE, A. L. *From Domesday Book to Magna Carta.* New York: Oxford Press, 1951.

PULLAN, LEIGHTON. *From Justinian to Luther.* Oxford: Clarendon Press, 1930.

DANIEL-ROPS, H. *The Protestant Reformation.* New York: E. P. Dutton, 1961.

HOLMES, GEORGE. *The Later Middle Ages.* New York: W. W. Norton & Co., 1962.

CHADWICK, OWEN. *The Reformation.* Baltimore: Penguin Books, 1964.

SYKES, NORMAN. *The Crisis of the Reformation.* New York: W. W. Norton & Co., 1938.

WHALE, J. S. *The Protestant Tradition.* Cambridge: Cambridge University Press, 1955.

OBERMAN, HEIKO A. (ed.). *Forerunners of the Reformation.* New York: Holt, Rinehart and Winston, 1966.

DURANT, WILL. *The Reformation.* New York: Simon and Schuster, 1957.

DICKENS, A. G. *The English Reformation.* New York: Schocken Books, 1964.

BICKNELL, E. J. *A Theological Introduction to the Thirty-Nine Articles of the Church of England.* London: Longmans, Green & Co., 1919.

MORE, P. E. and F. L. CROSS (eds.). *Anglicanism.* London: SPCK, 1935.

PAINE, GUSTAVUS S. *The Learned Men.* New York: Thomas Y. Crowell Co., 1959.

ROUTLEY, ERIK. *English Religious Dissent.* Cambridge: Cambridge University Press, 1960.

HILL, CHRISTOPHER. *The Century of Revolution 1603-1714.* New York: W. W. Norton & Co., 1961.

WAND, J. W. C. *The High Church Schism.* New York: Morehouse-Barlow, 1951.

SYKES, NORMAN. *The English Religious Tradition.* London: SCM Press, 1953.

HERKLOTS, H. G. G. *The Church of England and the American Episcopal Church.* New York: Morehouse-Barlow, 1966.

SIMCOX, CARROLL E. *An Approach to the Episcopal Church.* New York: Morehouse-Barlow, 1961.

ALBRIGHT, RAYMOND W. *A History of the Protestant Episcopal Church.* New York: The Macmillan Company, 1964.

DEMILLE, GEORGE E. *The Episcopal Church Since 1900.* New York: Morehouse-Barlow, 1955.

DAWLEY, P. M. *Chapters in Church History.* New York: Seabury Press, rev. ed. 1963.

——. *The Episcopal Church and its Work.* New York: Seabury Press, rev. ed. 1961.

SPENCER, BONNELL. *Ye are the Body.* West Park, N.Y.: Holy Cross Press, 1950.

HIGGINS, JOHN S. *One Faith and Fellowship.* New York: Seabury Press, 1958.

VAN DE POL, WILLIAM H. *Anglicanism in Ecumenical Perspective.* Pittsburgh: Duquesne University Press, 1965.

MANROSS, W. W. *A History of the American Episcopal Church.* New York: Morehouse-Barlow, 1935.

ADDISON, J. T. *The Episcopal Church in the United States.* New York: Charles Scribner's Sons, 1951.

GIBSON (ed.). *The First and Second Prayer Books of Edward the Sixth.* New York: E. P. Dutton, 1910.

SHEPHERD, MASSEY. *The Oxford American Prayer Book Commentary.* New York: Oxford Press, 1950.

HOOKER, RICHARD. *Ecclesiastical Polity* 2 vols. ("Everyman's Library") New York: E. P. Dutton.

CROSS, F. L. (ed.). *The Oxford Dictionary of the Christian Church.* New York: Oxford Press, 1957.

MOSS, C. B. *The Christian Faith.* New York: Morehouse-Barlow, 1943.

1220